TREKKING IN NEPAL

SUGGESTED WALKING ITINERARIES IN THE HIMALAYA

Antoine D'Abbundo

Consulting editor: Kerry Moran

LOCAL COLOUR

A CIP catalogue record for this is available from the British Library

Distributed in the United Kingdom and Europe
by Hi Marketing
38 Carver Road, London SE24 9LT.
Fax: (0171) 274-9160

Distributed in the United States by Seven Hills Book Distributors
Fax: (888) 777-7799

ISBN 962-217-425-6

Editor: Aruna Ghose
Consulting editor: Kerry Moran
Photography: Antoine D'Abbundo
Maps: Jean Zéboulon, Peter Tom Le Bas
Design: Philip Choi

Printed and bound in Hong Kong

Sacred stone, engraved with an image of the Buddha

TREKKING
IN
NEPAL

CONTENTS

Part One: Practical Information

Introduction

The verb 'to walk' is too inadequate when used in relation to a walk in the Himalaya. Therefore, it may be more appropriate to use the verb 'to trek' instead. 'To trek' is from the Afrikaaner term trekken, used by Dutch settlers to describe a journey especially migration by ox wagon. It has since entered the English language and means 'to walk a long distance usually over land such as hills, mountains or forests'.

Where, when and how to go trekking? What are the formalities that you have to go through? What equipment should you take with you? What are the basic health precautions? How do you prepare a first aid kit? You will find all the answers in this book, and more.

Many tourists confuse Kathmandu with Nepal while many trekkers consider their trip to Nepal as a 'physical adventure'. The objective of this guide is to give a general overview of a country which is not limited to its capital, no matter how beautiful, nor to its mountains, no matter how grand.

The Country

Situated between two giants, Tibet (under Chinese rule since 1951) to the north and India along the rest of its borders, Nepal has had a paradoxical history compared to the other countries in the region. It is, for instance, one of the only countries that has never been under any foreign rule, and is to date is still the largest Himalayan kingdom. A fact partly due to its geographical location.

THE HIGH MOUNTAIN KINGDOM

While the terrain is quite diverse, the topography of Nepal is rather simple. It is commonly divided into six large geographical regions, from the northwest to the southeast and from the south to the north.

The flat, narrow strip of land along the border with India is the Terai which forms part of the flood plains of the Ganges River. This humid and tropical region was until quite recently a barely habitable swamp, infested with the malaria mosquito. However, malaria has since been brought under control, the land has been cleared, and rice as well as sugarcane are now being cultivated on the Terai's fertile alluvial terraces. The Siwalik Range is an area of low range hills with a maximum height of 2,000 metres where forests prevail. Valleys here are called duns.

Further north, the Mahabharat Lekh Range or the Middle Hills (about 3,000 metres) is divided by a series of endless steep ridges formed by small streams.

Then comes the Pahar or Middle Country, also called the 'Nepalese middle plateau', but is in fact a region of low mountains (below 2,000 metres), cut by important valleys such as the Kathmandu or Pokhara valleys.

The high altitude region is dominated by the Himalaya. Throughout Nepal there are ten peaks measuring more than 8,000 metres (see page 14) and about 250 peaks measuring more than 7,000 metres. The highest mountains are found mostly in central and eastern Nepal.

However, this 'great wall' is not impassable. It is cut through, from the north to the south, by three of Nepal's most important rivers (the Karnali, Kali Gandaki and Sapt Kosi), as well as many smaller ones. In addition, there are twenty passes which enable one to cross over, on foot as well as by car, for instance through the Kodari Pass (1,663 metres), which via the Arniko Highway, links Nepal to Tibet.

Last but not least, in the northern part of the country is a region formed by a range of valleys and low mountains (around 6,000 metres). This region, called the Trans-Himalaya, is dry with a barren landscape similar to the Tibetan high-plateau. This region is not dominated by the monsoon which otherwise prevails over the rest of the country.

Facts And Figures

Size: 147,181 sq km (57 percent of Great Britain or 1.5 percent of the United States). Nepal is 885 kilometres long and 193 kilometres wide.
Capital: Kathmandu.
Population: 22 million. The population growth is about 2.4 percent per year. The average density is 118 inhabitants per square kilometre. 14 percent of the population is urban; 46.6 percent live in the Terai; 45.6 percent in the hills and only 7.8 percent live in the high mountains.
Official language: Nepali. Nepali is spoken by 59 percent of the population. There are over a dozen other languages and dialects spoken in Nepal, to name just a few: Maithili, Bhojpuri, Tharu, Tamang and Newari. Nepal's literacy rate is about 65 percent.
Religion: Hinduism. Nepal is the only country in the world where the state

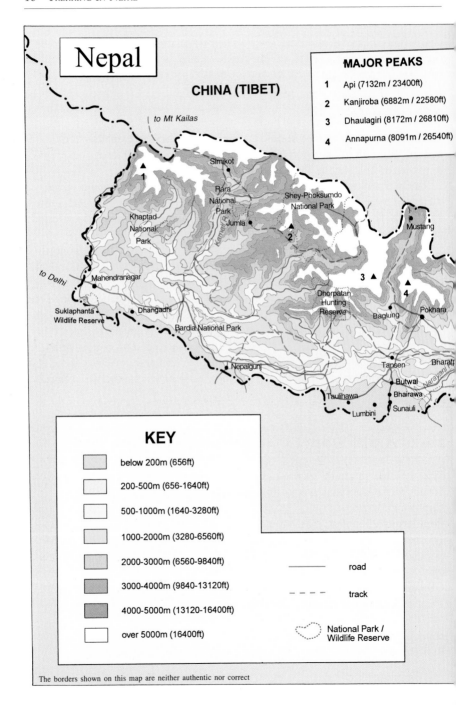

Nepal

CHINA (TIBET)

to Mt Kailas

MAJOR PEAKS

1 Api (7132m / 23400ft)
2 Kanjiroba (6882m / 22580ft)
3 Dhaulagiri (8172m / 26810ft)
4 Annapurna (8091m / 26540ft)

Simikot

Rara National Park

Shey-Phoksumdo National Park

Khaptad National Park

Jumla

Mustang

to Delhi

Mahendranagar

Suklaphanta Wildlife Reserve

Dhangadhi

Bardia National Park

Dhorpatan Hunting Reserve

Baglung

Pokhara

Nepalgunj

Tansen

Bharati

Butwal

Taulihawa

Bhairawa

Lumbini

Sunauli

KEY

below 200m (656ft)

200-500m (656-1640ft)

500-1000m (1640-3280ft)

1000-2000m (3280-6560ft)

2000-3000m (6560-9840ft)

3000-4000m (9840-13120ft)

4000-5000m (13120-16400ft)

over 5000m (16400ft)

——— road

- - - - track

National Park / Wildlife Reserve

The borders shown on this map are neither authentic nor correct

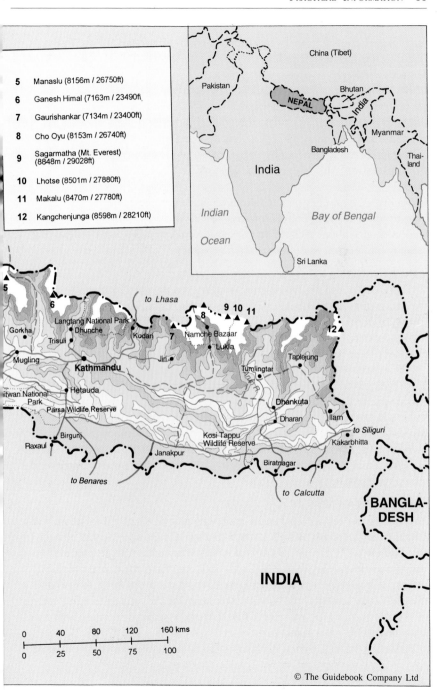

5 Manaslu (8156m / 26750ft)

6 Ganesh Himal (7163m / 23490ft)

7 Gaurishankar (7134m / 23400ft)

8 Cho Oyu (8153m / 26740ft)

9 Sagarmatha (Mt. Everest) (8848m / 29028ft)

10 Lhotse (8501m / 27880ft)

11 Makalu (8470m / 27780ft)

12 Kangchenjunga (8598m / 28210ft)

China (Tibet)

Pakistan

NEPAL

Bhutan

India

Myanmar

Bangladesh

Thailand

India

Indian Ocean

Bay of Bengal

Sri Lanka

to Lhasa

Langtang National Park

Gorkha

Dhunche

Trisuli

Kodari

Namche Bazaar

Lukla

Mugling

Jiri

Kathmandu

Tumlingtar

Taplejung

Hetauda

Chitwan National Park

Parsa Wildlife Reserve

Dhankuta

Dharan

Ilam

Birgunj

Raxaul

Janakpur

Kosi Tappu Wildlife Reserve

Kakarbhitta

to Siliguri

Biratnagar

to Benares

to Calcutta

BANGLA-DESH

INDIA

0	40	80	120	160 kms
0	25	50	75	100

© The Guidebook Company Ltd

religion is Hinduism. Nepal's population is about 88 percent Hindu, 7 percent Buddhist and 3 percent Muslim.

Money: The Nepalese rupee (written as Rs).

GNP: The per capita income is about US$180 a year. This makes Nepal one of the ten poorest countries in the world.

Political regime: Monarchy. The ruling king, Birendra Bir Bikram Shah Dev has reigned since 31 January 1972. (He was crowned in 1975 according to Vedic rituals and is still considered by the people as an incarnation of the God Vishnu.)

Administration: The country is divided into five regions, 14 zones and 75 districts.

Economy: Agriculture generates about 65 percent of the GNP and involves 86 percent of the working population. Arable soils comprise only 18 percent of the land. Although about 255,000 tourists visit Nepal annually, it is the Terai that actually produces most of the country's resources.

THE MONSOON

The summer monsoon phenomenon originates in the Bay of Bengal. Attracted by the depressions of the Tibetan high-plateau, warm and humid air streams follow the plains of the Ganges in a northwesternly direction until they meet the first high mountains. As a result, from mid-June until mid-September, heavy rains pour over these regions.

The impact of the monsoon varies greatly according to the altitude. It is mostly felt in the Terai, in the southern part of the country. In summer, the climate in the Terai is extremely hot, with heavy rainfall. There is hardly any cold season. In the central regions, there is a slight difference between summer and winter temperatures. Kathmandu, for instance, enjoys a temperate climate. In the Himalaya, the climate is obviously very cold, almost similar to arctic conditions. However, until an altitude of 4,000 metres, the contrast between summer and winter temperatures is still obvious.

THE RHODODENDRON KINGDOM

Altitude differences in Nepal create many different climates and therefore many different environments as well. In the Himalaya, for instance, at mid-altitude (up to 2,500 metres) there are subtropical forests where oak, walnut, pine and bamboo are found. Between 2,500 and 3,500 metres, is the domain of the temperate mixed forests or the kingdom of rhododendrons (with more than thirty different varieties) mixed with pine trees. Further up (up to 4,500 metres) the land is barren with few trees, while the higher peaks are covered with rocks, snow and ice.

However, this description of Nepal's vegetation is much more hypothetical than real and hardly takes into account the rapidly growing population. As mentioned before (see page 9), although a small number of people live in the mountains, they still need a lot of land. Over the generations, more and more hillsides have been totally stripped of its forests only to be replaced by terraced cultivations found all over the country.

Deforestation still continues as Nepal's forests provide most of the fuel used in the country. It has been calculated that about 25 percent of Nepal's forests have disappeared over the past ten years.

In Nepal, agriculture depends on altitude, since changes in altitude affect the climate and the people's lifestyle. Rice, for example, can only be grown up to an altitude of about 2,000 metres. Corn, wheat, barley and millet can be grown higher, up to about 3,500 metres. Higher up, people's diet depends upon summer-type cultivations such as buckwheat and potatoes.

Livestock (sheep, goats or yaks) are reared along with agriculture.

People From The North

The current population of Nepal is a mixture of distinct ethnic groups. Although it was officially abolished under the Constitution of 1962, the caste system, which originates from Hinduism, still largely influences Nepal's society.

Simply put, Hindu society is divided into superior or pure castes and inferior or impure castes. The various ethnic groups - mostly Buddhists - are considered as superior castes, although not as high as the Brahmans or the Chhetris, the highest castes in the system inherited from ancient India.

The Newars are the native inhabitants of the Kathmandu Valley (about 500,000 individuals) and have their own highly-structured caste system.

Most of Nepal's tribes belong to the Mongoloid type. Their languages belong to the Tibeto-Burman group while their culture is mostly Tibetan. These communities, who inhabit the higher Himalayan regions, are loosely termed Bhotia or Bhote (another word for Tibet). Their largely caste-free society is a totally different culture from midland Nepal's.

Tamangs (about 500,000) are the largest - and poorest - of the tribal groups. They live in the high hills to the east of Kathmandu and often work as porters.

Gurungs (180,000) are mostly farmers and stockbreeders. They live in the hills in central Nepal and enjoy a relatively high standard of living.

Thakalis (10,000) live in the high valley of the Kali Gandaki, a strategic commercial centre.

Finally, groups such as the celebrated Sherpas, who live in the northern part of the country (the Dolpo, Mustang and Manang regions), and in the east (the Solu-Khumbu and Everest areas), practise Tibetan culture and religion. They are expert trekkers and mountaineers.

The Ten Great Summits

Nepal possesses ten of the world's 14 peaks which measure more than 8,000 metres:

Everest: 8,848 metres, in Khumbu, towards the east of Kathmandu. Takes its name from the British geographer, Sir George Everest. It is known as Chomolungma among the Tibetans and Sagarmatha among the Nepalese. On 29 May 1953, it was conquered by Sherpa Tenzing Norgay and New Zealander Edmund Hillary.

Kangchenjunga: 8,586 metres, in Mechhi zone, at the border of Sikkim in India. Conquered in 1955.

Lhotse: 8,501 metres, on the southern side of Everest. Succumbed to the assaults of Peter Hillary, son of Edmund Hillary in 1956.

Makalu: 8,475 metres, in Kosi, towards the southeast of Everest. In May 1955, Jean Couzy and Lionel Terray hoisted the French flag on its summit.

Yalung Kang: 8,420 metres. Kangchenjunga's 'younger brother'.

Lhotse Shar: 8,383 metres. The 'eastern shoulder' of Lhotse.

Dhaulagiri: 8,167 metres, towards the west of the Kali Gandaki. 'Resisted' till 1960.

Manaslu: 8,163 metres, in central Nepal. A well-equipped team of Japanese mountaineers reached its summit in 1956.

Cho Oyu: 8,153 metres, in Khumbu, northwest of Everest. The first successful ascent took place in 1954.

Annapurna I: 8,091 metres, east of the Kali Gandaki. The first-ever peak measuring more than 8,000 metres to be conquered by man. The climbers were two Frenchmen, Maurice Herzog and Louis Lachenal.

Brief History Of Nepal

Very little is known of the early Licchavi and Thakuri dynasties. The first well-known dynasty, the Malla, was established in AD 1200 and lasted until 1768. King Jayastithi Malla (1382-1395), one of the greatest of Malla kings, established and codified the caste system based on the Indian model. Another great personality in Nepal's history was King Bhupatindra Malla (1692-1722), who built the fine Nyatapola temple-pagoda and the Bhadgaon temple. At that time, Nepal was divided into several small kingdoms, with the valley's three main cities, Kathmandu, Bhadgaon (Bhaktapur)and Patan, fighting and bickering all the time. These skirmishes enabled the Shah family, from the small kingdom of

Gorkha in central Nepal, to become the strongest power in the region. In 1743, Prithvi Narayan Shah, a born leader, became the ruler of Gorkha and launched his campaigns against the three kingdoms. Finally, in 1767 he conquered the valley and unified Nepal. However, battles continued until he died in 1775. Several political intrigues undermined this great dynasty which more or less gave Nepal its present borders.

In 1839, Jung Bahadur Rana appointed himself Prime Minister and he and his family virtually ruled Nepal for the next 104 years treating the country as their private estate. The Shah king's power was reduced and he became a mere puppet, even though he sat on the throne. For the next century the Shah kings were powerless pampered figureheads, indulged and kept out of politics. During this time, Nepal remained in almost total isolation, closed to outsiders.

After India's independence in 1947, pressure grew in Nepal for the Ranas to reform the government. Suddenly in 1950, King Tribhuvan fled to India, bringing a series of troubles upon Nepal. The end of the Rana regime was in sight. In 1951, King Tribhuvan returned to Nepal and within a year had taken control again of the country. After his death in 1955, his son King Mahendra ascended the throne. In 1958, he organised the country's first free elections and later established the first Constitution. However, democracy brought new frictions to the country and in 1962, King Mahendra resumed near control of the government. The text of the Constitution was amended in 1980 and is still in use since Birendra Bir Bikram Shah Dev became king on 31 January 1972, and remains on the throne, since 1991 as a constitutional monarch of a democracy.

The Religious Question

While most of the Nepalese follow a form of Hinduism, similar to that in India, the ethnic groups you will meet while trekking in Nepal are generally Buddhist. This kind of Buddhism finds its origin in Tibet, based on the teachings of the historical Buddha whose real name was Siddhartha Gautama, and who was born in the sixth century BC in Lumbini, now part of Nepal's Terai region.

Tibetan Buddhism is unique in the sense that it focuses on certain rituals such as the recitation of mantras (including the well known Om mane padme hum), circumambulations, prostrations, and the spinning of prayer wheels.

The monasteries or gompas are important centres of spiritual life. They often belong to one of the four main Tibetan schools (including the Dalai Lama's Yellow Hat School). Large festivals, such as the Mani Rimdu which celebrates the victory of Buddhism over Shamanism, usually take place in monasteries.

However, magical, animistic and shamanistic cults as well as superstitions still influence most aspects of everyday life.

Visas And Permits

Trekking in Nepal has become a kind of industry the country has come to rely upon. However, whether written or not, there are certain rules and regulations which you will have to comply with.What follows should help you select the trek most suitable for you:

FORMALITES

All foreigners, except Indians, who wish to enter Nepal must have a valid visa. Contact your local Nepalese embassy or consulate for information.

Australia: AMP Palace, 10 Eagle Street, Level 21, Suite 44, Brisbane, Queensland 4000 (tel: 07/232 0336)

Bangladesh: United Nations Road, Road No 2, Baridhara Diplomatic Enclave, Dhaka (tel: 2/601 1790)

Belgium: Avenue Franklin Roosevelt, 24, 1050 Brussels (tel: 32 (02)/ 649 4048)

China: No 1, Xi Liu, Jie, Sanlitun Lee, Beizing (tel: 086 (10)/ 532 1795)

Egypt: 9, Tiba Street, Dokki, Cairo (tel: 361 6590)

France: 45 Rue des Acacias, Paris 75014 (tel: 46/224 867)

Germany: 15 Im Haag, D 53179, Bonn (tel: 0228/343 097)

Great Britain: 12A Kensington Palace Gardens, London W8 4QU (tel: 0171/229 1594)

India: Barakhamba Road, New Delhi 110001 (tel: 11/383 484) Woodlands, Sterndale Road, Calcutta 700027 (tel: 33/452 024)

Italy: Piazza Medaglie d'Oro 20, 00136 Rome (tel: 06/345 1642)

Japan: 14-9 Todoroki, 7-Chome, Setagaya-ku, Tokyo (tel: 03/3705 5558)

Netherlands: 687 Gelderland Bldg., NL 1017 JV, Amsterdam (tel: 020/25 0388)

Pakistan: House No 506, Street No 84, Attaturk Avenue, Ramna G 6/4 Islamabad (tel: 5/821 0642)

Switzerland: P.O Box 8030, Zurich (tel: 01/261 5993)

Thailand: 189 Sukhumvit Soi 71, Bangkok 10110 (tel: 2/391 7204)

United States: 2131 Leroy Place, NW, Washington DC (tel: 202/667 4550)

Visa applications require a valid passport, one passport-size photograph, one duly filled application form (obtainable at the embassy or consulate). The visa fee has to be paid in cash – $15 for 15 days, $25 for 30 days.

Each visa is only valid for a single entry (to be used within three months following the application) and enables you to stay 30 days in Nepal. However, you can get an extension for a maximum duration of three months whilst you are in Nepal.

You can also apply for a visa upon arriving in Nepal from Tribhuvan Airport or from any border entry point.

Visa extensions have to be processed by the Immigration Office in Kathmandu (see map pages 18-19). Visa extensions require a valid passport and two passport-size photographs. Extensions cost US$2 per day after the stipulated 30 days.

In any case, a visa enables you to visit all areas of Nepal accessible by road primarily the two main valleys of Kathmandu and Pokhara and the southern part of the Terai. If you wish to travel further, into remote and mountainous regions, you will need to apply for a 'trekking permit'.

TREKKING PERMITS

The trekking permit is the trekker's 'real passport', the key that will open the door to the mountains.

To obtain a trekking permit, you must apply to the Immigration Office in Kathmandu located on Tridevi Marg (see map pages18-19); or in Pokhara in Simal Chaur (see map page 69).

Trekking permit applications require a valid passport, two passport-size photographs and an application form for the required region. Costs are calculated on a week-to-week basis and have to be paid in US dollars.

If the trek you have selected entails cutting across a National Park (which is often the case), an extra entrance fee of Rs650 has to be paid.

Applications for the trekking permit must specify not only the dates you wish to begin and end the trek but also the starting and finishing points. Any change in itinerary, especially if you enter restricted areas (usually mentioned at the back of the trekking permit), can be penalised with a heavy fine. However, if you respect the basic rules, checks (quite frequent) are just a mere formality.

Although the immigration offices may appear disorderly, they are actually quite efficient and organised. During the peak season you may have to stand in a queue for several hours before your application is processed, but trekking permits are usually delivered on the same day.

Warning: Do not let young Nepalese 'take care of everything' as some may offer to do so while you are queuing up. They are usually ineffective and just want to make a few extra rupees.

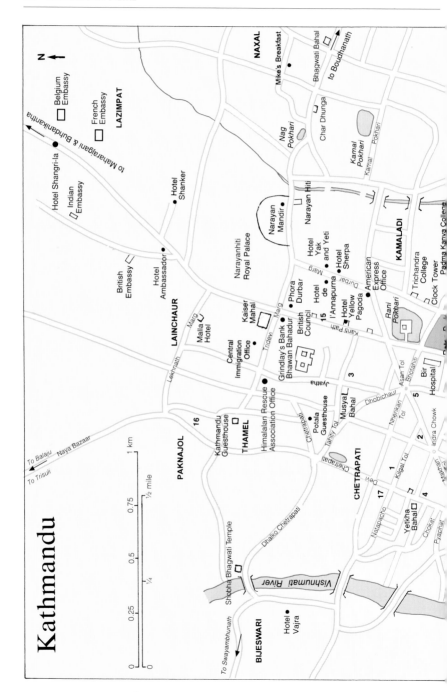

Kathmandu

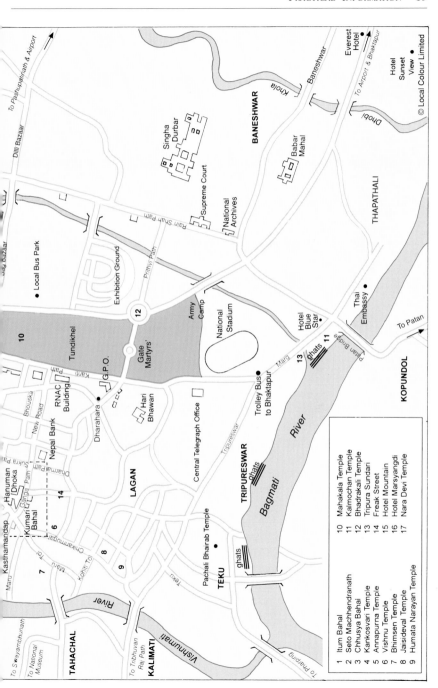

© Local Colour Limited

1 Itum Bahal
2 Seto Machhendranath
3 Chhusya Bahal
4 Kankosvari Temple
5 Annapurna Temple
6 Vishnu Temple
7 Bhimsen Temple
8 Jaisideval Temple
9 Humata Narayan Temple
10 Mahakala Temple
11 Kalmochan Temple
12 Bhadrakali Temple
13 Tripura Sundari
14 Freak Street
15 Hotel Mountain
16 Hotel Marsyangdi
17 Nara Devi Temple

Himalayan Rescue Association (HRA)

The Himalayan Rescue Association (HRA) is a Nepalese voluntary organisation registered with His Majesty's Government to run a mountain rescue service in the mountain tourist areas. It is located in Jyatha, near Thamel. It offers information and informative briefings on altitude sickness, essential if you're going to Khumbu or crossing a high pass like the Thorung La. Logbooks of comments from returned trekkers offer up-to-date advice on lodges, prices and trail conditions. The nearby office of the Kathmandu Environmental Education Project (KEEP) provides information on ecologically responsible trekking, and operates a small library, a coffeeshop, and a noticeboard for trekking partners.

How To Choose A Trek

As you must have probably guessed by now, before applying for a trekking permit you should know where to go, when to go and how to go.

WHERE?

For a long time, in fact until the early fifties, Nepal remained closed to foreigners. Yet, for unknown reasons, the situation is still more or less the same today as entire regions of the country are still 'forbidden' to tourists. However, interior borders are slowly opening up. Nowadays, travel agencies specialise in organising treks and suggest new routes that go through formerly restricted regions such as Mustang or Dolpo, or even Kangchenjunga (at the border with Sikkim in India). Although these regions do have the potential to attract a lot of trekkers in the future, at present they are still very rough. Lack of roads, absence of reliable maps and inadequate accommodation arrangements can turn trekking in these regions into large-scale operations, accessible only to the very rich or the very adventurous.

The itineraries you will find in the second part of this book are the 'classics' - the Everest Base Camp, the Annapurnas, sacred Gosain Lake, the Langtang Valley, Helambu and to some extent Rara National Park. These sites are not only extremely beautiful but are also very safe: all along their routes there are shelters or 'lodges' where for a small amount of money travellers can eat and sleep. There are numerous villages and emergency help is always available, sometimes even by helicopter. Providing proper attention is given to planning these itineraries, they can be undertaken alone.

To choose your itinerary, read the introduction to each trek. Each introduction provides information on the length of the trek, its main difficulties as well as its main points of interest.

WHEN?

The best time to go trekking depends, of course, on your destination. Here we have divided the itineraries into two types:

Mid-range treks (up to 3,500 metres). Can be undertaken any time of the year. However, try to avoid the monsoon season from mid-June until mid-September. These itineraries include:
- From Pokhara to Jomosom.
- Helambu.
- From Jiri to Namche Bazaar.
- From Jumla to Lake Rara.

High altitude treks (3,500 metres and above). Again try to avoid not only the monsoon months but also the winter (from December to February) as the cold is dreadful, the snowfall very heavy and some of the passes are blocked. These itineraries include:
- The Annapurnas and their surroundings.
- The Annapurna Sanctuary.
- Gosain Kund and Langtang.
- The Sacred Lakes of Gokyo.
- Everest Base Camp.

In any case, the best time of the year to go trekking in Nepal is from September to November, and from March to May, when the days are sunny, the rhododendrons are in bloom, and the snow mountains have their best visibility.

HOW?

Going through a travel agency is by far the easiest and most popular way to organise a trek. You just have to indicate where you want to go and the agent will take care of everything. He will also deal with formalities such as trekking permits, insurance, transportation etc. A team usually includes several porters, a chef or 'kitchen boy', and a *sirdar* or 'guide-interpreter'. The team has a very rigid hierarchy where each individual knows his exact role and each day functions according to a very strict routine.

Departure is early. While you are still having breakfast, some of the porters will dismantle the camp and leave so that they can reach the next site before you and begin to prepare lunch. The others will patiently wait while you finish your breakfast and pack the rest of the luggage which they will carry. In the evening, you will find that the camp has been set up and tea ready. All you have to do is... walk. Some will enjoy not having anything to do. Others may find this lack of activity tedious.

Another drawback is the cost. The daily package depends upon the agency, the destination, the kind of services you request and the number of trekkers. Prices usually range from US$30 to 50 per person, per day.

Also, unless you are already travelling with a group of friends, you may have to join a group of other trekkers, which may or may not be a good idea.

It is almost impossible to provide a comprehensive list of trekking agencies. There are a number of them in Kathmandu though some open or close down almost every day.

However, for those trekkers who would like to carry their own bags, who for financial or other reasons prefer to make their own arrangements or wish to go trekking with friends, it is possible to organise your own trek, and although it will obviously require more effort, this guide is here to help you.

Equipment

You must remember that to trek is above all to walk and that even if you reach very high altitudes (Kala Pattar in the Khumbu region is 800 metres higher that Mont Blanc, the highest European peak), it is not necessary to carry any specialised mountaineering equipment. However, neither is it advisable to go under-equipped wearing only a sweater and a pair of sneakers.

SHOES
Suitable shoes are the trekker's best friends. They must be stout as well as comfortable, keep the feet and ankles secure and also be waterproof. Many brands and different models are available in the market now. The question is for you to find a suitable pair. The price of a good pair of walking shoes is about US$40 or more. Do not wear a pair of brand new shoes at the beginning of a trek as it is a sure way to end up with painful blisters. It is also advisable to keep an extra pair of lightweight shoes which will be a pleasant change for the evenings as well as a back up in case of an emergency.

RUCKSACKS
You won't need a rucksack if you have decided to organise your trek through a travel agency. The porters that the agency have hired for you will carry your luggage. Traditionally, Nepalese porters carry their load in large rattan baskets called *doko* strapped around their forehead so that the weight is split between the

back and the nape of the neck. For Nepalese porters, a rucksack is therefore of little use, even to the pint of being rather cumbersome and inconvenient. A large travel bag or a duffel bag is more suitable since you will be able to lock it, making it much safer.

If you are going to carry your own bag, a rucksack is obviously the best solution. A rucksack must be strong, waterproof and practical, preferably with internal and external pockets and a separate compartment for a sleeping bag. Its capacity should be at least 60 litres. Pay particular attention to details such as the waist-belt or the shoulder straps which will make it easier to carry.

To pack a rucksack is a skill. Here are a few tips on how to make it as balanced and easy to carry as possible: don't cram everything down at the bottom of the bag; roll your clothes so that they occupy less space; wrap clothes in plastic bags to avoid humidity (also very useful later as laundry bags); use socks to fill in the gaps. Again do not forget that getting the correct balance is the secret of a properly packed rucksack.

SLEEPING BAGS

The trouble with buying a sleeping bag is that it is difficult to find one that combines the right weight/durability/price ratio. A down-filled sleeping bag can be as warm as a synthetic one; it is lighter, but also more expensive. The internal material has no real bearing on how warm it is, but it can make a difference in terms of weight. Although it is heavier, cotton is more comfortable than synthetic.

To make it easier, buy the right sized sleeping bag, preferably a "mummy bag", ie one that is (body-hugging and with a hood), with a shoulder strap and a pad/draught excluder along the zip for greater protection against the cold.

Essential Equipment

Equipment
- Rucksack
- Sleeping bag
- Water bottle
- Torchlight (plus spare bulb and batteries)
- Map and compass
- Multipurpose knife
- Survival blanket
- Lighter or matches/candles
- Toilet paper (almost all the lodges sell some)
- Emergency kit (see next chapter)
- Waterproof wallet
- Sunscreen

Clothing
- Sunhat
- Sunglasses
- Jacket with hood
- Polar jacket or sweater
- Raincoat
- Long sleeved T-shirt
- Underwear (take quite a few pairs. Although the weather may be cold one tends to sweat a lot)
- Walking socks (take quite several pairs of these too. Better to carry some extra weight rather than spend the whole time washing socks)
- Walking shoes
- Towels and swimsuits

In winter or in high altitude
- Windproof trousers
- Hat and gloves

Supplemental Equipment

Equipment
- An small backpack (for one-day excursions or for those who travel through an agency)
- Tent (usually unnecessary, except for a few destinations mentioned in this book. If needed, they can be rented in Kathmandu)
- Foam mattress (for those who cannot sleep without one or for those who want to sleep outside)
- Gas cooker and utensils (heavy and cumbersome. Gas cartridges are not found in Nepal, nor can they be carried on the plane)
- Walking stick

Clothing
- Sneakers (it's such a relief to take off your walking shoes)

Miscellaneous
- Camera (don't forget to buy the film and batteries to go with it before you leave.)
- Personal stereo/radio (plus a few tapes. Nepalese radio broadcasts news in English every evening. You may be lucky enough to receive it)
- Books (buy them before you leave or in Kathmandu)
- Notepad (writing a diary in the evening by the fireside is a favourite pastime of trekkers)

Money.......

Apart from large towns like Kathmandu and Pokhara, and certain stopovers such as Jumla, Jomosom and Namche Bazar, it is difficult to find any banks. This means that you will have to carry a lot of cash with you. It is not easy to specify the exact amount, Rs500 per day seems reasonable considering the low rates 'lodges' ask for accommodation and food (Rs50 per night and Rs150 maximum for a meal). Even so, it is still a substantial amount of cash to carry around. Bank notes come in denominations of 1,000, 500, 100, 50, 25, 20, 10, 5, 2 and 1 rupee notes. A different colour distinguishes each from the other and the amounts are written in both Nepalese and English. Don't forget to keep some small change handy. A cup of tea will cost somewhere between two and five rupees so try to avoid paying with a Rs100 note.

Tipping is on the increase in Nepal. Trekking staff rely on tips to boost their meagre salaries. A good rule of thumb is US$1-2 per trekking day per group member, to be divided among the trekking staff, with the sirdar and cook at the top of the list. Porters are tipped on the last day of the trek, perhaps one day's extra salary per week of the trek.

It is wise to divide your money and stash the portions in different places so that you don't lose any or have all your money stolen at one time. A little pouch to carry around your neck is probably the most secure. You may want to carry a few US dollars which you should be able to change, if necessary, with a lodge owner. But beware of the exchange rate! Travellers' cheques can be useful in case you need to buy a plane ticket, but don't forget your passport.

TO BUY OR TO RENT?

Investing in brand new equipment may not be possible for certain trekkers. Some shops in Kathmandu, Pokhara and Namche Bazaar sell or rent second-hand equipment, usually bought from previous expeditions. Prices are usually lower than in Europe, and the quality/price ratio is quite good. The challenge is to bargain.

To really protect you from the cold as well as to allow you to sleep safely and soundly in any season, a sleeping bag should be able to combat temperatures as low as minus five to ten degrees.

Health

One need not be an athlete or a skilled mountaineer to trek in Nepal. But you must remember that walking for several days in the mountains is demanding and requires some amount of physical fitness. There are a few rules one should respect both before leaving and during the trek.

The most common ailment that affects trekkers is diarrhoea. The one that must be taken the most seriously is altitude sickness, also called Acute Mountain Sickness (AMS). A full paragraph is dedicated to this problem and we strongly advise you to read through it carefully.

You should also be aware that there are very few health care centres available in the mountains (see sidebar list). It is therefore very important that the first aid kit you carry with you is as comprehensive as possible. At 4,000 metres, a small 'boo boo' can become a real hassle. In a separate sidebar, we suggest a list of medicines you should take with you and it may be a good idea to ask your own general practitioner to help you put it together according to your medical needs.

Before The Trek

No matter how old you are, and even if you are perfectly healthy, it is wise to have a medical check-up before you leave. It is even more advisable to do so if you suffer from chronic diseases such as asthma or diabetes. To visit your dentist may not be a bad idea, since tooth cavities tend to occur with the altitude. Make sure your international vaccination certificate is up-to-date. If not, update it and if you have not been vaccinated, this is the best time to do so. That may take some time since all the vaccinations cannot be administered at the same time.

Although no special inoculations are required to obtain a Nepalese visa, protective measures against poliomyelitis, tetanus and diphtheria is advisable. Again, make sure your vaccinations are up-to-date. It is also advisable to be vaccinated against typhoid and rabies. Cholera is not very widespread in Nepal so vaccination is not necessary. Another protective measure to consider is the new vaccination against Hepatitis A, effective for ten years. To date there is no effective vaccination against malaria, which still prevails in the remote areas of the Terai. The best way to avoid it is to deprive mosquitoes of the opportunity of biting you by covering up properly and using effective repellants and coils.

Physical exercise is of course the best way to prepare oneself. For the duration of the trek, your body will be under considerable stress caused by the continuous effort, the climate, the different heights and uncomfortable living conditions. These changes may be drastic so to be in good physical condition is really the best protection against illness or accident.

DURING THE TREK

There are three major hassles most trekkers will have to face in Nepal: the cold, diarrhoea and leeches.

During the trekking season the days are usually nice and sunny. However, in the mountains, temperatures can vary rapidly. For example, from May to October, at a height between 1,000 and 3,500 metres, the average temperature is 20 degrees celsius during the day, but it can drop to 5 degrees at night. Under such circumstances, catching a cold is easy. Often, trekkers do catch colds because they have not brought the right equipment (see previous chapter on equipment) or because they have neglected basic precautions like walking without wearing a hat (most of the evaporation takes place on the head), or by not slipping into dry, warm clothes during even the short breaks.

Eating contaminated food or drinking polluted water may bring on an attack of diarrhoea, so it is important to be careful without becoming paranoid. The best way to prevent a bad attack is to avoid fresh vegetables and fruits and only drink water that has been boiled for at least five minutes. You can also add a tablet of Micropure to the water you drink from your flask. This and other brands are available at chemists. The tablets should be kept in the water for at least an hour before they are effective. Avoid food that has been left standing out and unboiled milk.

Leeches are very common during the monsoon season from mid-June to mid-September. Unfortunately, there is no known 'leech repellent' . One 'old wives' tale' is to apply salt on those parts of the body like the feet, ankles, neck and armpits, where leeches tend to 'make themselves at home'. If you find one, don't panic! These little beasts are disgusting but they are harmless. It is not necessary to burn them - as is commonly said - to remove them as you may burn yourself as well! You can just pull them off with a stick or with a pinch of salt. Clean and disinfect the wound carefully and use plaster to prevent any infection.

Acute Mountain or Altitude Sickness

Every year, a number of travellers suffer from high altitude or Acute Mountain Sickness (AMS). It can be very serious and even fatal because of the ignorance of its causes, symptoms and remedies.

__Its causes:__ The higher the altitude, the lower the atmospheric pressure. Gases become less dense and the availability of oxygen in the atmosphere diminishes. In order to face these changes, the human body has to adjust. If the ascension of the mountain is too fast for the body to adapt, the person may develop one or several symptoms of altitude sickness, the most serious – and sometimes fatal – being pulmonary or cerebral oedema.

__Its prevention:__ Trekking above 2,500 metres involves the risk of altitude sickness, especially if one has not taken the appropriate precautions. The best way to avoid such discomfort is to get acclimatised to the altitude. Sensible precautions include:

1) Climbing up progressively. From 2,500 metres, it is advisable not to climb more than 500 metres a day;

2) From 3,500 metres, it is advisable to spend a night or two at each stage;

3) Drink plenty of fluids. A minimum of two litres a day is recommended above 3,000 metres to counteract dehydration. Avoid alcohol or sedatives.

__Symptoms and remedies:__ Even if you follow these rules it does not mean that you will not suffer from any of the symptoms. Each person has a different level of tolerance to altitude and there are no established rules. Therefore, it is important to pay attention to even the most minor symptoms which include headaches, dizziness, loss of appetite, nausea, insomnia, shortness of breath, urine retention and oedema.

The only remedy for severe symptoms is to climb down as soon as possible. You can take medicines such as Diamox, but with caution as it may simply mask the warning signs of AMS. Trekkers who experience mild symptoms can try remaining one or two days at the same altitude, before resuming their ascent at a measured pace.

For more information, ask the Himalayan Rescue Association in the Thamel area of Kathmandu (see map of Kathmandu page 18) which is open from 11 am to 5 pm every day except Saturday. The HRA runs two health care centres in the mountains (see page 32)

First Aid Kit

Essentials
Small pair of scissors, a pair of tweezers, safety pins, bandage, plaster, sterile compresses (20 x 26 cm), disinfectant, aspirin or paracetamol tablets, water purifying tablets.

Prescriptions
Decongestion medicine, painkillers, anti-spasmodics, massage cream for contusions and sprains, Diamox (a mild diuretic which stimulates oxygen intake, used to treat mountain sickness), multi-purpose antibiotics.

Extras
For comfortable feet - plasters to protect against blisters, talcum powder (to spread into socks and shoes), antibiotic cream, suntan lotion, lip balm, mosquito repellent, chewable vitamin C tablets, ear plugs, glucose bars for regaining energy.

Health Care Centres

In Kathmandu
The following list is obviously not exhaustive. In any case, before you leave it is better to apply for a special travel insurance that includes repatriation.

CIWEC Clinic, Yak & Yeti Road (off Darbar Marg), tel: 228 531
Nepal International Clinic, Hitti Durbar, tel: 419 713
Patan Hospital, Lagankhel, tel: 522 266

During The Trek
Remember that most of the health care centres listed below have limited equipment and staff. You will only find basic treatment here. In case of a serious problem, the Nepal Air Force can provide assistance and use its helicopters, but only if you can guarantee payment! If you know someone in Kathmandu, it may be a good idea to ask for him/her to be your guarantor. Emergency assistance is expensive and can cost up to US$1,200 to US$2,000. In case of emergency you can send a radio message from one of the administrative offices.

In the Everest region: In Jiri - a small hospital; in Lukla - a health care centre; in Namche Bazar - a small clinic; in Khunde - the Hillary Trust Hospital; in Pheriche - an emergency centre run by the Himalayan Rescue Association (HRA). Open during the trekking season only.

In the Annapurnas: In Besi Sahar - a dispensary; in Chame - a health care centre; in Manang - an emergency centre run by the HRA during the trekking season only; in Jomosom - a small hospital; in Tatopani - a health care centre; in Ghandrung - a dispensary run by the Annapurna Conservation Area Project (ACAP); in Pokhara - a modern hospital.

In the Gosain Kund, Langtang and Helambu regions: In Trisuli Bazaar - a hospital ; in Dhunche - a dispensary; in Langtang - a health care centre. Please note that no health care centre is available in the Helambu region.

In the Rara region: In Jumla - a hospital; in Gumghadi and Bota - a dispensary.

Lord Ganesh, protector of travellers

Food and Drink

Dal bhat. Nepal's national dish: A lentil curry (*dal* means 'lentils' in Nepali) mixed with *bhat* (rice), accompanied with spicy green vegetables (a kind of spinach) or potatoes. Meat is rare, especially in the mountains but you can sometimes find poultry prepared with spices or masala. Dal bhat is eaten as a single dish – Nepalese rarely eat starters or desserts – and is served 'unlimited'. A porter can eat up to one kilo of rice a day. Westerners eat much less and generally tire easily of this healthy but rather boring diet.

CHAPATI
A kind of unleavened bread often baked in the fireplace. Excellent for breakfast.

TSAMPA
Traditional dish, the base of which is barley flour mixed with a spicy soup or tea. Can also be mixed with sugar and butter. Very filling and energizing. Will advantageously replace cereal bars.

MOMOS
Small, steamed or fried dumplings stuffed with vegetables or meat.

SHERPA STEW
Sherpa soup prepared with mixed vegetables, noodles and sometimes meat. Ideal in cold weather.

RIGI KUR
Grated potatoes prepared on the grill and accompanied with hot pepper and butter. Above a certain altitude the potato becomes the staple food as it can be prepared in a thousand different ways, including the simplest ones - steamed or cooked in ashes.

INTERNATIONAL DISHES
Most of the lodges offer some sort of international dishes like spaghetti Bolognese or yak steaks with french fries which you commonly find on the menus.

You can also buy eggs, as well as other dairy and grocery products (milk, biscuits, chocolate, instant soup, etc). Before you buy tinned food, check the 'best before' date which is likely to have expired. Whatever be the menu that you decide on, try to make it for the whole group, so your host does not waste wood.

WATER
Unless you treat it (see the chapter on Health, page 28) it is better not to drink water from the streams, ponds or from the village water taps. You will find mineral water in all the lodges, however before buying, make sure the top is

sealed and check the 'best before' date. As such bottles are carried by porters up the mountains, their price varies greatly according to the altitude you buy them at. From Rs20 in Kathmandu to Rs100 up... Also don't forget that plastic packagings are highly polluting. Burn them if you are camping or carry them back with you.

TEA

Chiya in Nepalese. Ask for 'kalo chiya' if you want it black, with or without sugar; and ask for 'dudh chyia' if you drink it with milk. The Tibetans and other mountain communities prepare it with salt and mix it with yak butter. Very healthy but tastes funny. However, if you like it, tea is a comforting drink. In addition, there is no risk of contamination since the water has to be boiled.

CHANG

The local beer. Brewed from rice, corn and cereals. Each household has its own secret method of brewing. The level of alcohol varies accordingly. Traditionally, the glasses should be filled again and again until the bottle is empty.

RAKSI

Similar to chang but much stronger. A good raksi must first go through fermentation and then through at least five or six processes of distillation. Transparent, it looks and tastes a little like Japanase sake. Can be drunk pure, warm, or mixed with an egg or with butter. Better be prepared.

TONGBA

Comes from the fermentation of millet added to hot water. Drunk from large jugs through bamboo straws.

OTHER DRINKS

Nepal produces now, under international licence, some good quality beer that can be found almost anywhere. The price is quite steep though like Coca-Cola, it can be bought at the base of Mount Everest.

Part Two: Itineraries

This section describe seven general itineraries. Why only seven, you may ask. Well, because each of them describes much more. The itineraries we have selected in fact combine several smaller and easier walks. We have also suggested 'loop' treks to avoid walking back in your tracks. For 'beginners' as well as for trekkers in a rush we have indicated 'short cuts', whereas for the 'experts' the routes are more difficult and cross high altitude passes. The reader can select the most suitable one based on his or her ability. To help you make your choice, each itinerary is accompanied by a small locater map, followed by a general map of the route as well as a table indicating the difference in altitude on a day to day basis. Each stop is described in detail - roads, population, scenic views, lodges, etc. We have tried to be as precise and detailed as possible, but remember - things change very fast in Nepal. Each year, new lodges open, others close down, prices change and so does the landscape and names of places. Sometimes, even altitudes differ from map to map! These discrepancies are unavoidable and reiterate that mountains can never be conquered.

I)   AROUND THE ANNAPURNAS

II)   THE ANNAPURNA SANCTUARY

III)   GOSAIN KUND, LANGTANG AND HELAMBU

IV)   FROM JIRI TO NAMCHE BAZAAR

V)   EVEREST BASE CAMP

VI)   GOKYO LAKES

VII) FROM JUMLA TO LAKE RARA

Corbelled bridge above the Marsyangdi River, on the way from Jagat to Dharapani.

Around The Annapurnas

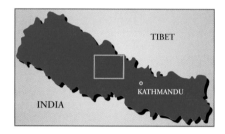

Introduction

A complete tour of the Annapurnas is undoubtedly one of the most popular treks in Nepal, yet it is also the most controversial. Some people refer to this route as a 'highway' because of the large number of tourists one encounters during the peak season from September to November.

Unfortunately the critics are justified. However, it would be a pity to forfeit the joys of walking and discovering some of the country's highest and most spectacular mountains - the Annapurnas, Lamjung, Manaslu, Nilgiri, Dhaulagiri and Machhapuchhare are just some of the peaks the itinerary attempts to cover. The trek also goes through diverse terrain, from the subtropical forests of the lower Marsyangdi to the dry valleys of the Mustang, from the Thorung La to the meandering Kali Gandaki.

The culture shock is equally impressive. Nepal is a mosaic of peoples and you will meet Brahmans, Tamangs, Gurungs, Thakalis, Magars, and of course, Tibetans, who have all settled in the shadow of Annapurna, revered locally as the Goddess of Abundance.

Tourism has benefitted some of the population. Greater wealth has led to more commerical attitudes and it is likely that some people will want to see the contents of your wallet before extending any hospitality. But for most of the inhabitants life is still pretty tough, yet their smiles are genuine and devoid of any materialistic motives. These are the persons worth meeting.

It is important to choose the right time to visit. March, April and May are the most appropriate months as the climate is favourable (after the heavy winter snows when the peaks are impenetrable and before the excessive monsoon rains when the pathways are waterlogged). There are fewer tourists as well at this time. The following itinerary covers 18 days, the minimum number required to get acclimatised at your own pace. However, trekkers in a hurry have the option to follow part of the itinerary - from Dumre to Jomosom for instance, and then catch the flight back. Or from Pokhara to Jomosom, and return the same way. The itinerary runs from the east to the west. The reason for this is that until 1993 the route crossed the Thorung La from Manang. Today, there is a lodge between Muktinath and the Thorung La which means that trekkers do not have to climb about 1,600 metres on the same day. If you decide to leave from Pokhara, read the suggested itinerary in the reverse order, but remember - it is quicker to climb downhill than to climb up!

For The Tough Guys

If you do not want to drive from Dumre to Besi Sahar, you will have to walk along the Marsyangdi River for 18 kilometres up to Turture (526 metres) where you can spend the first night. The following day, cross the suspension bridge at Tarkughat (on the eastern side). Once on the west side, keep walking up to Paundi (579 metres). Follow the road going through Syubar, Bhote Odar and Udipur (747 metres) before going down to Phalenksangu (716 metres). From here, the track goes up and down until Besi Sahar, crossing several rivers which are tributaries of the Marsyangdi.

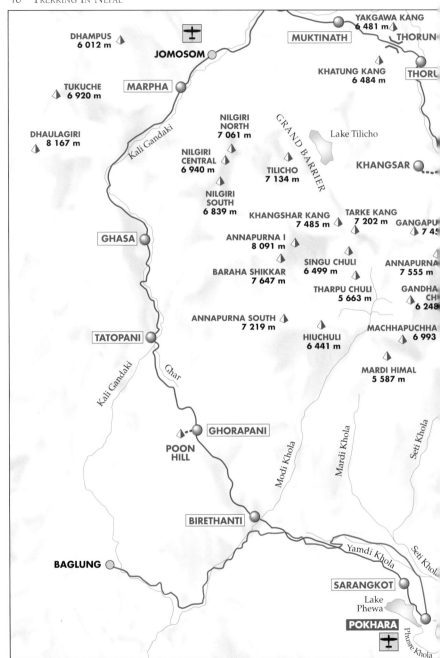

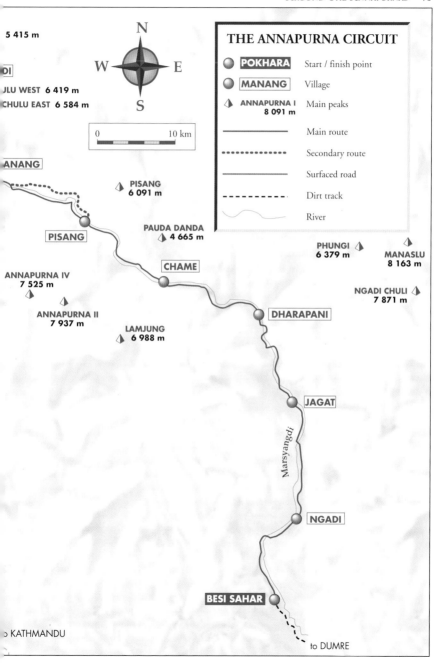

5 415 m

JLU WEST 6 419 m

CHULU EAST 6 584 m

ANANG

ANNAPURNA IV
7 525 m

ANNAPURNA II
7 937 m

THE ANNAPURNA CIRCUIT

POKHARA   Start / finish point

MANANG   Village

ANNAPURNA I
8 091 m   Main peaks

———————   Main route

· · · · · · · · · · ·   Secondary route

———————   Surfaced road

– – – – – – –   Dirt track

~~~~~   River

PISANG
6 091 m

PAUDA DANDA
4 665 m

PISANG

CHAME

PHUNGI
6 379 m

MANASLU
8 163 m

NGADI CHULI
7 871 m

DHARAPANI

LAMJUNG
6 988 m

JAGAT

Marsyangdi

NGADI

BESI SAHAR

KATHMANDU

to DUMRE

The First Day

FROM KATHMANDU TO BESI SAHAR (bus: about 10 hours)
You will need to travel for about ten hours, first by bus and then by truck, to cover the 173 kilometres or so from the capital, Kathmandu, to the village of Besi Sahar, where the trek starts. Two types of regular public transportations - the 'local bus' and the 'tourist bus'- connect the Kathmandu Valley with the Pokhara Valley towards the west.

If the tourist bus is more expensive, it is also faster and much more comfortable. We suggest that you buy your tickets from one of the many travel agencies in Thamel in Kathmandu, the day before your departure at the latest. For the price, you can make a reservation and secure a numbered seat (try for one of the front seats which are usually less crammed). You will thus avoid travelling on top of the bus, with the luggage and sometimes livestock, as often happens to the more haphazard traveller. Buses usually leave early in the morning from Kanti Path Avenue, near Grindlay's Bank (see map of Kathmandu, pages 18-19), and take a little over four hours, including stopovers, to cover the 136 kilometre-highway between Kathmandu and Dumre village. From Kathmandu, the bus follows the Tribhuvan Highway in the southwest direction until Naubise. The stretch of the highway leading to the Chandragiri Pass is a series of winding curves and twists over bumpy, uneven surfaces. This, with the never-ending traffic, makes this part of the journey very uncomfortable, more so since it takes at least an hour and a half to cover less than 30 kilometres.

From Naubise, the route follows the Prithvi Highway along the Mahesh Khola (River), until it meets its confluent, the Trisuli Khola, in the village of Simpani. The road then runs along the south bank of the river, one of Nepal's best river rafting locations, up to the village of Mugling. The Trisuli and the Marsyangdi rivers meet here to become the Narayani River, also called the Sapt Gandaki, one of the tributaries of the Ganges. Usually the bus stops for lunch just before Mugling after which it takes another hour to reach the village of Dumre, 26 kilometres away, which is the entry point to the Manang Valley. For sometime, treks used to start from this rather dull village, located at a height of 457 metres. While some trekkers still like to use Dumre as their base camp, most prefer to go by truck to Besi Sahar. The truck schedule is quite irregular (it does not start until it is full of passengers), the fees are 'negotiable' (the average rate for a tourist is about Rs80, but it could be more) and the road is bumpy. Try to get a seat inside the front cabin where at least you can sit, rather than in the main body of the truck, which has no seats at all. You will thus avoid two hard days of walking along a track which very often follows the road anyway (see sidebar).

After the four or five hours spent in covering 37 kilometres you will reach Besi Sahar (823 metres), the main town of the Lamjung district. Until recently, this market town of 2,000 inhabitants was called Besigaon. However, since the opening of the road to Manang, in the late-seventies, the village became a compulsory stopover for those who go trekking around the Annapurnas and was renamed Besi Sahar. You will find several administrative offices here, as well as a post-office and a police checkpost where your trekking permit will be examined for the first time. Check in at the Tukuche Peak Hotel, which is right opposite the truck station. This simple lodge offers individual rooms at reasonable prices. During summer ask for a bed with a mosquito net. From the garden the view of Mount Lamjung is splendid. Next door, The Thorung Guest House is more modern but expensive, while the Annapurna Lodge is rather noisy.

The indispensable trekking permit - expect to pass through at least ten checkposts.

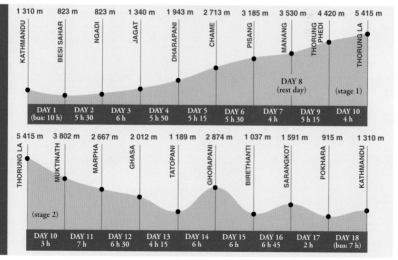

The Second Day

From Besi Sahar to Ngadi (about 5 hours 30 minutes)
Walk across the village heading northwards, until you reach the District Forest Office. Then climb down for 150 metres, heading towards the Pam Khola on the other side of a small bridge. The track then goes up again till the hamlet of Sanuti (or Chanaute), less than thirty minutes away.

The track (about 100 metres high) then overlooks the west side of the Marsyangdi. After about an hour of walking across fields of paddy, barley and corn as well as pockets of subtropical forests, you will come across the river again at the small village of Bhalam, where there are several teahouses or bhattis. Here, an old suspension bridge crosses the Marsyangdi - keep to the left bank. It will take you another hour before you find the suspension bridge which crosses the Khudi Khola to reach one of the region's first Gurung villages. Khudi (792 metres) offers a great variety of lodges and small restaurants where you can have lunch.

At the end of the village, you will find a high school. For another hour follow the track running along the west side of the Marsyangdi until you reach the suspension bridge at Bhulbhule (853 metres). Cross over. Ngadi Chuli Peak (7,871 metres), also called Manaslu II or Peak 29, is visible to the right. After the lodges, the track follows the eastern bank of the Marsyangdi, and after less than an hour of walking amidst plantations of rice, corn and millet you will reach Sharude hamlet. On the way, several scenic points will give you the chance to admire Manaslu Peak (8,163 metres) and Ngadi Chuli to the northeast.

Walk for another hour to reach Ngadi village (860 metres), sometimes spelt as Ngatti in certain maps. There are several lodges here, of which the Himalaya Lodge and Restaurant, just at the beginning of the village, is clean, has a nice arbour and is perfect for dinner.

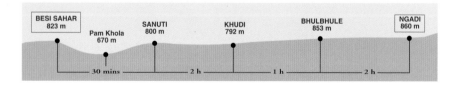

(Previous spread) The suspension bridge at Bhulbhule.

The Third Day

FROM NGADI TO JAGAT (about 6 hours)
Head towards the north up to a suspension bridge crossing the Ngadi Khola. At this point, the track on the right leads to the village of Usta. The path going up towards the Marsyangdi leads to the village of Lampata in the Manang district. The climb is quite steep and it takes about two hours to reach Bahundanda, a village sitting on a headland at a height of 1,314 metres. Bahundanda means 'Brahman's hill' which explains the origin of its people. It is an ideal stop for lunch and to enjoy the view of Mount Phungi (6,379 metres), towards the north. From Bahundanda, climb down a rather steep slope for about thirty minutes until you reach the Dhule Khola, cross over to reach the village of Besi. The track, through fields of corn, overlooks the east side of the Marsyangdi. It then crosses the Tatopani Khola and after a short, steep rise, reaches the hamlet of Lili, about thirty minutes away. It takes another thirty minutes of easy walking above the Marsyangdi, before reaching Kanigaon. Soon you will see the magnificent waterfall at Syange (1,136 metres) flowing from the high plain hamlet of Ghiluma. From here, use the suspension bridge to cross the Marsyangdi again and turn to your right (usually there is a sign that indicates the road to Manang). The path on your left leads to the waterfall. After a short climb (about fifteen minutes), the track enters a gorge shaded by rhododendrons and wild hemp. Thirty minutes later, you will reach the hamlet of Shree Chomu, from where it will take another hour to reach Jagat, a village built along the ridge of the mountain, at a height of 1,340 metres.

At the end of the village you will find the Manaslu Lodge, our favourite because of its proximity to the hot springs. These cannot be used in summer though because of the rise in water level.

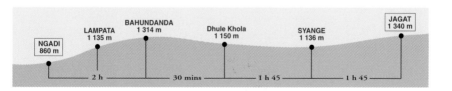

The Fourth Day

FROM JAGAT TO DHARAPANI (about 5 hours and 50 minutes)
From Jagat, it takes thirty minutes to climb down to the banks of the Marsyangdi River which is very deep at this point. After ascending for about forty five minutes, you will reach a bhatti, from where it will take another thirty minutes to reach the village of Chamje (1,433 metres). Another ten minutes will take you to a suspension bridge that crosses the east bank of the Marsyangdi. The track edges its way through huge rocks before it slowly heads upwards, sometimes quite steeply. After an hour's climb, you will reach the hamlet of Sattare ('top of the hill', in Tibetan), a traditional stopover for porters and an ideal place to have lunch. After Sattare, the track follows the ridge of the hills for about thirty minutes and then climbs up through a bamboo forest, for another hour, to the village of Tal set in the middle of a broad valley. At the top of the hill, about fifteen minutes before Tal, stands Danfe Lodge at the border between the Lamjung and Manang districts.

The entrance to Tal (1,707 metres) - tal means 'lake' - is indicated by a kani, a kind of arch made of stones, which is a common sight in the region. In the village, your trekking permit will be checked once again by the local police. You will also find several lodges and some shops selling handicrafts manufactured in ... Kathmandu.

From Tal, it takes fifteen minutes to reach the hamlet of Siranthan and then another ten minutes to reach a crossing indicated by stones. Take the path on your left, it will lead to a corbelled bridge that you will have to cross to reach the west side of the Marsyangdi. The path then climbs up to the hamlets of Nigale Kakh and Hotoro. From here you can see the old and now abandonded path on the other side of the river.

After Hotoro, you will have to return to the east side of the Marsyangdi, crossing the bridge at Karte village. You will still have to walk for at least thirty minutes before you can reach Dharapani (1,943 metres), which means 'stream'. Just before the village, you will have to cross the river once again. Check in at either the Dharapani Hotel or Ganga Jamina Hotel. The latter offers a splendid view of Mount Phungi towards the east.

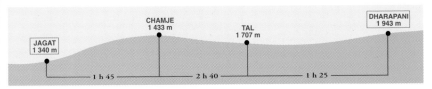

Mount Phungi, as seen from Bahundanda.

The Fifth Day

FROM DHARAPANI TO CHAME (about 5 hours and 15 minutes)
If you follow the west bank of the Marsyangdi from Dharapani (make sure you
do not take the bridge leading to Thonje), it will take about forty five minutes to
reach the village of Bagarchap (2,164 metres) which literally means 'the river
bank'.

This is where the Marsyangdi curves to flow in an east-west direction.
Bagarchap marks the barrier between the humid valleys of the south that you
have just crossed and the dry regions of the high-Marsyangdi. That the monsoon
is more or less absent in this region is evident by the change in vegetation.
Instead of subtropical forests there are large tracts of blue pine, oak and spruce.
Between the gaps, there are views of Mount Lamjung (6,988 metres) and
Annapurna II (7,937 metres) to the southeast, and Manaslu or Ngadi Chuli to
the east.

From Bagarchap, it will take an hour to climb up to the hamlet of Dhanagyu
(2,300 metres) where you can stop for lunch. After you have passed the Na
Khola first and then the Chauri Khola, which falls into the Marsyangdi as a
gigantic waterfall, you will reach the village of Tamang Besi, about an hour away.
The path then continues to ascend to Latamarang, which stands at an elevation
of about 2,350 metres.

A trek of an hour and forty five minutes through the hamlets of Thanchock
and Besi Salla Chari (which means 'the garden of pines') will take you first to
Koto (sometimes spelt Kodo, meaning 'millet'), and then to the village of Kyupar
(2,600 metres). Outside the village, a police checkpost controls the access to the
Nar Phu Khola Valley which leads to Tibet, still out of bounds to foreigners. You
will have to show your trekking permit here again. Chame (2,713 metres), the
district headquarters of Manang district, is another forty five minutes away. All
the government administrative offices of the region are located here which is
probably the reason for its lack of charm. The only attractions are the views,
though partial, of Mount Lamjung and Annapurnas II and IV (7,525 metres). Of
all the lodges, our favourite is the Danfe Hotel, the largest in town and also the
most comfortable and reasonably priced.

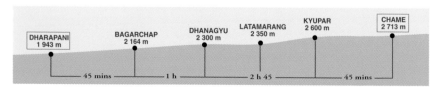

The Sixth Day

FROM CHAME TO PISANG (about 5 hours and 30 minutes)
Soon after the school at Chame, cross a bridge to get to the northern bank of the Marsyangdi. It takes about two and a half hours of walking along the river to reach the village of Bratang (2,919 metres), mainly populated by Tibetans. This is where you should stop for lunch. From Chame to Bratang, the path goes through a splendid pine forest and offers unparalleled views of Lamjung and Annapurnas II and IV. Some maps still show the old path which once crossed the Marsyangdi River two times over, an exercise that is not necessary anymore, so stick to the north side of the river as this new itinerary suggests.

However, about an hour after you have left Bratang, you will have to cross another suspension bridge. The altitude here is about 3,000 metres and you can see the Pauda Danda, a gigantic rock that overlooks the river from a height of 1,500 metres.

Once you have crossed the bridge, you still have to climb a ridge for about an hour. Once on top, trekkers traditionally plant a pine sapling, not only to establish that they have made it to the top, but also to contribute to the reforestation of the area.

Climbing down to Pisang (3,185 metres) takes about an hour. There is not a single house on the way, nor will you find any water.

The village of Pisang is divided into two sections - the lower and the upper villages. All the lodges are located at the base of the valley, to the south of the Marsyangdi. The upper village, which is also the main one, is on a hillside on the other side of the river. The climb up, although hardly more than a hundred metres, is exhausting especially after a rather tough day. Nevertheless, it is worth the effort – for the charming wooden houses with their fretted windows as well as for the 360-degree view from the top of the hill that stretches from the Annapurnas in the south to Mount Tilicho (7,134 metres) in the west; and from Chulu East (6,584 metres) to the peak of Mount Pisang (6,091 metres) towards the north.

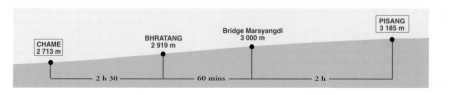

The Seventh Day

FROM PISANG TO MANANG (about 4 hours)
To go from 'lower' Pisang to Manang, trekkers have a choice of two itineraries. One runs along the north bank of the Marsyangdi, at an altitude of about 3,600 metres, and offers several climbs up and down. Though much longer and tougher it is also more exciting. If you decide on this itinerary, you first have to cross the river, then take the path on the left leading up to the village of Ghyaru (3,673 metres). Follow the ridge of the hill up to Ngawal (3,650 metres) and then climb down to the village of Mungji (3,350 metres), from where you can join the main itinerary which is described in detail.

The main itinerary, on the other hand, follows the floor of the Marsyangdi along its southern bank. After you have crossed the Pisang Khola, there is a forty five minute climb up a rather steep pass. From the top, however, you can catch glimpses of Pauda Danda (4,665 metres), Mount Pisang and the Manang Valley with, right before you, Mount Tilicho. After a quick walk down, it will take you another hour of walking across flat terrain to reach Hongde airport from where you can catch the occasional flight to Kathmandu. You can have lunch at one of the many bhattis and restaurants as well as have your trekking permit examined at the police checkpost.

After Hongde, the valley gradually widens. Annapurnas III and IV (7,555 metres and 7,525 metres respectively) are to the left, while to the right, although further away, are East and West Chulus (6,584 metres and 6,419 metres). Towards the horizon, there are views of the highest peak of Mount Thorung (6,481 metres), and to the east, the crown of Mount Pisang. After Mungji, the path crosses the Marsyangdi River once more and continues to the ancient village of Braga (3,505 metres). The entire route from Hongde takes about 90 minutes.

Braga is definitely worth a break in journey to wander through the picturesque village with its flat roofed houses and to visit the gompa, not only the largest in the region but also the richest with fine collections of thangkas (religious scroll paintings) and prayer books. Moreover, it only takes forty five minutes to walk from Braga to Manang, which sits on a plateau at 3,530 metres, so you can afford to take your time.

You may find that the prices in Manang are slightly higher than they are elsewhere. However, considering the quality of service, the prices are still fairly reasonable, even during the peak season. Our favourite lodge is the Tilicho Hotel, about a hundred metres from the kani, and near the medical centre. A double room will cost approximately Rs100 and the menu is a welcome break from the eternal dal bhat (rice with lentils).

(Top) Mount Pisang, one of the most popular peaks for trekkers.
(Previous spread) The Annapurnas as seen along the route from Chame to Pisang.

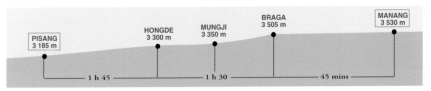

PISANG 3 185 m	HONGDE 3 300 m	MUNGJI 3 350 m	BRAGA 3 505 m	MANANG 3 530 m
— 1 h 45 —	— 1 h 30 —		— 45 mins —	

A view of Pauda Danda.
The 'upper' village of Pisang.

Manang Valley with Mount Tilicho in the horizon.
Manang village, overlooking the Marsyangdi River.

The Eighth Day

AROUND MANANG

Before you proceed towards the Thorung La pass, it will be wise to take a day off and explore Manang village and its environs to become acclimatised to the higher altitudes (see chapter on Health and Altitude Sickness, pages 28-31).

While Manang itself is of little interest, its surroundings are worth exploring - one of the most popular walks leads to a crest to the north of the village, which offers a panoramic view of Annapurna IV and Annapurna II to the southeast; and Gangapurna (7,455 metres) and Tarke Kang or Ice Dome (7,202 metres) to the southwest.

You can also cross the Marsyangdi and climb the impressive yellow rock pillars which dominate the south of Manang village. From the top you will catch a glimpse of the glacial lake lying at the foot of the northern slope of Gangapurna.

The more adventurous can walk further west up to the village of Khangshar, on the way to Tilicho Lake, where you will find the 'Great Barrier', discovered by the French explorer, Maurice Herzog, who climbed the first 8,000-metre peak when he conquered Annapurna I (8,091 metres) in 1950. The walk to Khangsar takes the whole day, so carry a picnic with you.

A glacial lake at the bottom of Gangapurna.

The Ninth Day

FROM MANANG TO THORUNG PHEDI (about 5 hours and 15 minutes)
After leaving Manang, the path climbs above the Marsyangdi Valley and leads to
the Jargeng Khola, one of the Marsyangdi's tributaries, which flows in a northeastern direction. Soon you will reach the hamlet of Tengi (3,642 metres), fifteen
minutes away. The path still climbs up across rocky terrain and it takes about an
hour to reach Gunsang (3,850 metres) where you will find a few bhattis.

Thirty minutes after Gunsang, you will cross a small river running down the
slopes of Gungdang and Chulu West, on the left. Climb for another hour to
reach the hamlet of Churi Lattar (sometimes spelt as Letdar), which stands at
4,250 metres. You can have lunch here at, for instance, the Yak Kharka Lodge.
These Himalayan pastures are the domain of the yak, a bovine of Tibetan origin,
reared for its wool, milk and to transport goods. The tahr, a kind of wild goat
that lives in herds, is also found here.

An hour's walk along the east bank of the Jargeng Khola leads to a small
bridge across the river. Walk up along a scree-covered slope. It is then a steep
climb of an hour and a half to reach Thorung Phedi (phedi means 'foot of the
hill'), sitting at 4,420 metres on a small hill overlooking a high plateau. This is
where you will find the last – and only – lodge before the Thorung La pass.

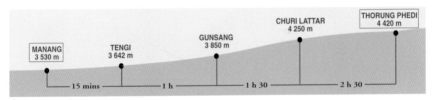

The Tenth Day

FROM THORUNG PHEDI TO MUKTINATH (about 7 hours)
The track above the lodge rises and climbs over a hill, the first of many that lead
to the pass. There are in fact twenty hills, we counted them, a little game that
helps endure the four or five hours it will take to reach the 5,415-metre-high
summit. On the way you will find several cairns (small mounds of rocks) and
prayer flags. This path is very popular during the peak season and you will not
get lost, except in winter, if the snowfall is heavy. Then, even if the rates (almost
Rs700 per day) sound prohibitive, the services of a local guide may be necessary.
We suggest that you leave early enough to reach Thorung La just as the sun rises.
You will thus avoid the 'rush hour' and also enjoy the magnificent scenery –
weather permitting – in peace and solitude. Framed by Yakgawa Kang or
Thorungse (6,481 metres) to the north, and Khatung Kang (6,484 metres) to the
south, the Thorung La offers wonderful views of the Annapurnas and
Gangapurna to the southeast. In the horizon to the west, Dhaulagiri (8,169
metres) and Mount Tukuche (6,920 metres) are also visible.

The descent towards Muktinath takes another three hours. The 1,600-metre
difference in altitude makes this section very strenuous. Fortunately, just a
couple of hours away from the pass (at about 4,000 metres), the new lodge,
which opened in 1993, is an ideal place to take a break and have lunch. Afterwards, the slope becomes gentle. You will then have to cross both a small gully,
caused by a temporary river, and a rocky plateau before you come to a Hindu
temple, very popular among pilgrims. The temple is only ten minutes away from
the oasis of trees that is Muktinath, even though it stands at 3,802 metres.

Once you reach the village, you will have to get your trekking permit in-
spected once more at the local police station. Check in at the Shree Muktinath
Hotel, one of the last hotels at the end of the village, near the North Pole Hotel.
From your bedroom you will have a splendid view of Dhaulagiri. You will also
have a chance to take a hot shower - fortunately there is electricity! Last but not
least, the menu offers a variety of international dishes. A good way to end a good
day!

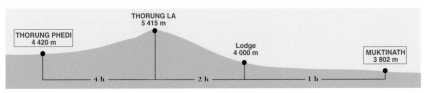

The Thorung Phedi Lodge, the last and only one before the Thorung La.

(Top) Thorung La, with the Annapurnas (to the southeast).
(Bottom) Dhaulagiri (to the west) and the village of Muktinath.

The Eleventh Day

FROM MUKTINATH TO MARPHA (about 7 hours)

Soon after you have crossed the hamlet of Ranipauwa, adjacent to Muktinath, you will reach the village of Jharkot (3,612 metres), mainly populated by Tibetans. For about an hour, the track goes down along the southern bank of the Jhong Khola until it reaches Khingar. It then continues, for another hour, across semi arid, rocky terrain, the habitual route of pilgrims and horse caravans, until Kagbeni (2,807 metres).

Situated at the confluence of the Jhong Khola and the Kali Gandaki, the village of Kagbeni, with its imposing, ochre-coloured gompa, has for a long time been 'the end of the world' for trekkers. Today, it is in fact the entrance to the Lo Monthang (or Mustang) region, which has recently been opened to tourism. There are several lodges here where you can have lunch.

After Kagbeni, the track heads towards the northeast/southwest following the Kali Gandaki River Valley (which literally means 'the black meanderer'), several hundred metres wide at certain points. Framed between the Annapurnas and Dhaulagiri, the valley is swept by strong winds in the morning which may make progress difficult. Sometimes you will see 'prospectors' examining round, black stones, in search of prehistoric ammonite fossils, called saligrams, a symbol of Vishnu. Such fossils are commonly found in souvenir shops in Kathmandu. Along the way do not forget to look at the superb views of the Nilgiris towards the southeast.

It will take you about two to three hours from Kagbeni to reach Jomosom (2,713 metres), the administrative headquarters of the region. Here, you will find an airport (with regular connections to Pokhara), a bank, post-office, hospital and a few hotels. The place is quite prosperous and has all the trappings of a garrison town which does not add to its charms. After you have gone through the inevitable police check, we suggest that you carry on walking until Syang (thirty minutes away), and then on to Marpha (2,667 metres), another hour away. With its black-slated streets and unusual architecture, this charming village is well worth the effort. It is also famous for its apple liquor.

Although not as luxurious as those in Jomosom, some of the lodges in Marpha, such as the New Dhaulagiri Hotel or the Baba Lodge, are very friendly and reasonably priced.

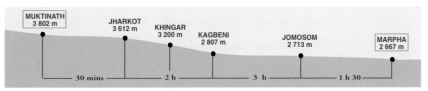

The Kali Gandaki River Valley with the entrance to Mustang in the horizon.

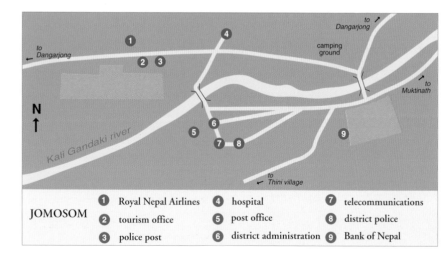

JOMOSOM

❶ Royal Nepal Airlines	❹ hospital	❼ telecommunications
❷ tourism office	❺ post office	❽ district police
❸ police post	❻ district administration	❾ Bank of Nepal

The Twelfth Day

FROM MARPHA TO GHASA (about 6 hours and 30 minutes)

From Marpha, walk along the west bank of the Kali Gandaki for an hour and a half to reach Tukuche (2,951 metres), dominated by the peak of the same name which stands at a height of 6,920 metres. This very beautiful village is populated by Thakalis, whose houses reflect just how significant this centre of trans-Himalayan trade is. Just before the public square, there is a signpost indicating the itinerary to Mount Dhampus (6,012 metres), one of the peaks a trekker can climb in Nepal.

After Tukuche, the path meanders along the Kali Gandaki River Valley for about an hour until it reaches the village of Khobang (2,550 metres). The village of Lajung (2,560 metres) lies thirty minutes away. Outside the village there is a giant pine tree where villagers sacrifice chickens and goats to propitiate the Goddess Kali.

The hamlet of Sokung (2,951 metres) is another thirty minutes later. Soon, you will have to ford a tributary of the Kali Gandaki, the Bhotsi Khola or 'the fierce river', so called because of the suddenness with which it rises. By climbing its opposite bank, you will soon reach a large suspension bridge above the Kali Gandaki. Cross it and in ten minutes you will reach the small village of Koketani. From here it takes another thirty minutes to reach the hamlet of Dhampu where you will have to cross the river again before entering Kalopani (or 'black water') located at 2,530 metres. Have lunch at this village and enjoy impressive views of Dhaulagiri, the Nilgiris (South: 6,839 metres, Central: 6,940 metres and North: 7,061 metres) and Annapurna I (8,091 metres).

From Kalopani to Lete (2,438 metres), a few minutes' walk will take you to the police station for yet another check. The descent is quite steep until the bridge across the Lete Khola, then the path climbs up and down over a low altitude tropical forest. It takes two hours to reach Ghasa (2,012 metres), another Thakali village.

You can check in at the Dhaulagiri Lodge and from its verandah observe the activities of the village.

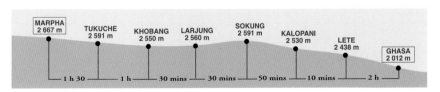

The Thirteenth Day

FROM GHASA TO TATOPANI (about 4 hours and 15 minutes)
After Ghasa, it will take you thirty minutes to reach a bridge leading to the
eastern bank of the Kali Gandaki. After the hamlet of Panoi Thala, fifteen minutes later, you will reach Deorali, the border hamlet between the Mustang and
Myagdi districts. Go down to the village of Kopchepani and walk up to the banks
of Kali Gandaki. After crossing several hills, the descent continues until a bridge
leading to the west of the river. A few minutes later, you will reach the village of
Rupse Chhara (1,550 metres), near a huge waterfall, an ideal spot for lunch.

From Rupse Chhara, it takes fifteen minutes to reach the village of Titar (also
spelt Titre), and another thirty minutes until Dana (1,446 metres), distinctive
because of its large houses with decorative windows. If you turn back after you
have crossed the Ghatte Khola, you can catch
a glimpse of Annapurna South (7,219
metres), or Annapurna Dakshin in Nepali.
From Dana, it takes about an hour and a half
to two hours of easy descent to reach
Tatopani (1,189 metres). The name of the
village means 'hot springs' for which the
village is famous. The hot springs, located on
the west bank of the Kali Gandaki, have a
relaxed atmosphere where both trekkers and
people from Kathmandu like to spend a few
days.

You can check in at the Namaste Lodge, in
the centre of the village, which has a pleasant
verandah and a garden of orange trees. Be
careful as the prices seem to rise rapidly,
especially during the peak season.

A young Nepalese going to the market in Pokhara.

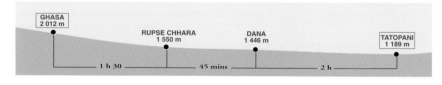

GHASA 2 012 m	RUPSE CHHARA 1 550 m	DANA 1 446 m	TATOPANI 1 189 m
1 h 30	45 mins	2 h	

The Fourteenth Day

FROM TATOPANI TO GHORAPANI (about 6 hours)
While the earlier itinerary from Kagbeni used to head in a north-south direction
and went down to the Kali Gandaki, it now goes east towards the Pokhara Valley.
It also moves from an area where Thakalis are the dominant population to enter
a region populated by Magars. With a difference in altitude of nearly 1,700
metres, this will be a hard day.

Fifteen minutes after Tatopani, you will reach a suspension bridge which
crosses the Kali Gandaki, soon followed by another bridge across the Ghar
Khola. A signpost erected by the Ministry of Tourism indicates the itinerary to
Ghorapani, which starts from a steep path on the left.

After an hour's climb up this path, you will reach a pass with a few bhattis and
a restaurant called the Top Hill Santosh, from where you can view the marvellous
panorama. The ascension then becomes slightly more gentle, but you will still
need about thirty minutes to reach the village of Ghara (1,768 metres) and
another hour to reach the village of Sikha (1,920 metres) where you can stop for
lunch.

The climb, through terraced cultivations, continues for about an hour and a
half to nearly two hours until Chitre (2,316 metres), and then across a rhododendron forest until Ghorapani, which is about an hour away.

Ghorapani (2,874 metres), which means 'watering place for horses', is, in fact,
a stopover for donkey caravans travelling from Jomosom to Pokhara and several
lodges are located here. You can check in at the Snow View Hotel in the middle
of the village, or even better, at the Hill Top View Lodge on the way to Poon Hill,
located at more than 3,200 metres, which offers magnificent views of Dhaulagiri,
Tukuche, the Nilgiris and Annapurnas I and South.

For details of the panorama from this particular spot, read the twelfth day of
the Annapurna Sanctuary Trek (see page 94).

Climbing to the top of Poon Hill takes about one to two hours. Start early in
the morning to make sure that you have a clear day when you reach the top.

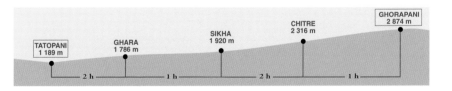

The Fifteenth Day

FROM GHORAPANI TO BIRETHANTI (about 6 hours)

After you have gone through the inevitable ritual at the police checkpost, start going down through a subtropical forest. On the way, which takes approximately an hour, you will meet several pony caravans. According to local belief, leeches, very common during the monsoon, are repelled by smell of ponies (see chapter on Health, page 28). You will soon reach the village of Nayathanti (2,450 metres) which is inhabited by the Magar tribe, traditionally recruited by the British army to serve in the Gurkha regiment. From here it takes another hour to reach Banthanti (2,250 metres). At the end of the village you can stop for lunch at the Fishtail Good View restaurant, which not only offers delicious dal bhat but also magnificent views of Machhapuchhare (6,993 metres) to the northwest. Nepalese regard Machhapuchhare or 'fishtail' as a sacred mountain because it is yet to be conquered by man.

After Banthanti, the forest disappears only to be replaced by terraced cultivations that spread up to the village of Ulleri, about thirty minutes away. You then have to climb down a path cut into a flight of steps for about two hours - very strenuous for your thigh and knee muscles. You will first reach the village of Tirkhedhunga (1,577 metres), followed by the village of Hille (1,524 metres), about fifteen minutes away. The descent is easier till you reach the banks of the Bhurungdi Khola. Follow the north bank along the villages of Jagarda, Ramkhoi, Randuari and finally Birethanti (1,037 metres). This Thakali village owes its prosperity to the fact that it is an integral part of both the trek from Pokhara to Jomosom and the trek to the Annapurna Sanctuary (see page 72).

Most of the lodges in Birethanti are managed by a committee which establishes the annual rates for the different hotel categories. The rate for a double room is fairly cheap. Check in at the New River Hotel, just before the bridge over the Modi Khola, or at the New Fish Tail Hotel, just after the bridge. For more luxury, you can try Laxmi Lodge. Prices are high but they are still pretty reasonable for the comfort and hospitality offered.

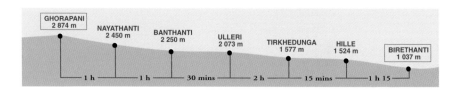

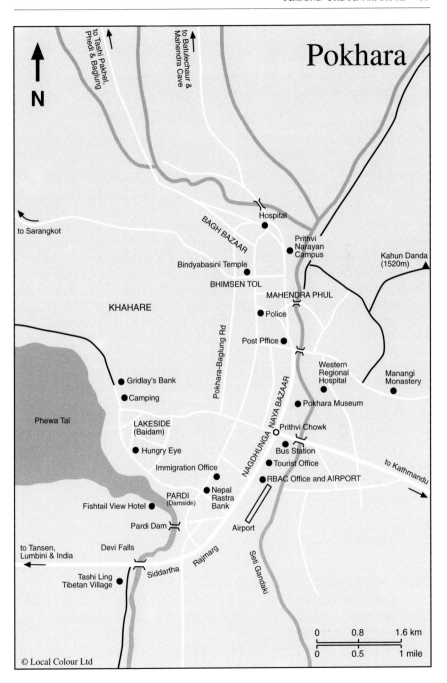

N

to Tashi Pakhel,
Phedi & Baglung

to Batulechaur &
Mahendra Cave

Pokhara

to Sarangkot

BAGH BAZAAR

Hospital

Prithvi
Narayan
Campus

Kahun Danda
(1520m)

Bindyabasini Temple

BHIMSEN TOL

MAHENDRA PHUL

KHAHARE

Police

Pokhara-Baglung Rd

Post Pffice

Western
Regional
Hospital

Manangi
Monastery

Gridlay's Bank

Camping

Pokhara Museum

Phewa Tal

LAKESIDE
(Baidam)

NAGDHUNGA NAYA BAZAAR

Prithvi Chowk

Hungry Eye

Bus Station

Immigration Office

Tourist Office

to Kathmandu

PARDI
(Damside)

Nepal
Rastra
Bank

RBAC Office and AIRPORT

Fishtail View Hotel

Pardi Dam

Airport

to Tansen,
Lumbini & India

Devi Falls

Rajmarg

Seti Gandaki

Siddartha

Tashi Ling
Tibetan Village

0		0.8		1.6 km
0		0.5		1 mile

© Local Colour Ltd

Many trekkers end the circuit here. The new Pokhara-Baglun road passes a half hour south of Biretanthi. Buses and taxis leave from Naya Phul, returning to Pohara in a little over two hours. Or you can choose to prolong your adventure by walking back to Pokhara over the old trekking route.

The Sixteenth Day

FROM BIRETHANTI TO SARANGKOT (about 6 hours and 45 minutes)
After you have crossed the Modi Khola, take the path heading up to Chandrakot (1,563 metres) on your left at the end of the village. This mule track is quite long and steep, sometimes cut into a flight of steps, and its ascension may take up to two hours. However, once you reach the top you will appreciate the effort. The vista includes Annapurna South and Machhapuchhare in the background, with a road, the first sight of 'civilisation', built with Chinese help between Pokhara and Baglung. It is better to have lunch here as the other surrounding villages do not have much to offer.

It will take another forty five minutes to reach the Gurung village of Lumle (1,615 metres). Here you will find the road that you will have to follow for about an hour before you reach Nagdanda (1,425 metres), a large market town without much interest. About a hundred metres after the police station, leave the road and take a path on your right heading towards Kaski Kot. Two to three hours of easy climb, amidst fields of corn and millet, is necessary to reach the village of Sarangkot (1,591 metres). You will notice that each village has its own pokhari or 'small pond' which is the place where cattle come to bathe.

If you have the time and energy - and weather permitting - you can walk up to the television transmitting station overlooking Sarangkot, from where you can have your last glimpse of Machhapuchhare, with the Pokhara Valley, on the opposite side, to the east.

The Seventeenth Day

FROM SARANGKOT TO POKHARA (about 2 hours)
The descent is through a pathway cut into steps, which runs first amidst pastures and then through a rhododendron forest, until Phewa Tal or Pokhara Lake. Follow its banks to reach the city centre.

Situated at 915 metres, Pokhara is the country's second largest city, located on the west bank of the Seti River, which at this point flows through very impressive gorges. The town has a Royal Residence as well as a luxury hotel, the Fishtail View Hotel, both sitting on the banks of the lake. Near the airport you will find the immigration office where you may want to have your trekking permit verified or extended. From the airport runway, the panorama is grand - the entire Himalayan range stretches for about 50 kilometres, right before you.

It is possible to rent a bike to explore the town and its surroundings. There are dozens of hotels and restaurants to choose from. We recommend the Amrit Lodge, in the Baidam area, by the lake. The rates for an individual bungalow with a private bathroom is not more than Rs300 during the off season. Quite reasonable for a town where the price inflation for tourists otherwise has no limit.

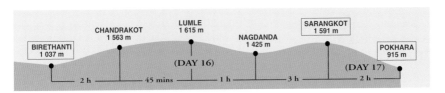

The Eighteenth Day

FROM POKHARA TO KATHMANDU (Bus: about 7 hours)

There are two ways to leave Pokhara:

1) By plane. The price for foreigners is US$61. RNAC, Everest Air, Nepal Air, Lumbini Airways, Buddha Air and NECON Air all fly between Pokhara and Kathmandu. Try to get a seat on the left hand side of the plane to enjoy the panorama of the Himalayan range for the final time.

2) By bus. You should book your seat the day before you plan to leave at the latest. The return trip also takes seven hours.

THE ANNAPURNA SANCTUARY

Introduction

Once you have walked along the pathways leading to Pokhara (often called 'New Switzerland' in certain tourist brochures) you will understand why a trek to the Annapurna Sanctuary is deemed essential among trekkers in Nepal. The trail, which leads from the banks of the scenic Lake Phewa to the sacred forest of Jode Yehm, entails walking from terraced rice fields to snowy peaks in just a few days. Such diversity is typical of Nepal, and seldom found anywhere else in the world.

Consequently this trek is very popular, especially between the months of September and November when the route can get very crowded. During winter the number of trekkers reduces as walking in the mountains is both difficult and hazardous because of the heavy snowfall. Avalanches are also common particularly along the last section of the route. The monsoon or rainy season (from mid-June to mid-September) is equally perilous. The most suitable period is therefore from end-February to end-May when the weather conditions are favourable and there are fewer people.

Some trekkers do accomplish this itinerary in less than ten days. But this is only possible if you stick to the Modi Khola Valley, and if you don't lose your breath.

The itinerary that we describe here is a loop itinerary and demands at least fifteen days. It partly joins the Around the Annapurnas Trek as we think a 'detour' through the villages of Ghorapani and Tatopani is really worth the time and effort. However, for those in a hurry we also suggest an alternative itinerary that will save three days.

In general, the main route has no major difficulties. The average altitude is 3,000 metres and even the highest point, that of the base camp of the Annapurnas, does not exceed 4,000 metres. A string of villages line the route, each almost adjacent to the other, and most of the lodges you come across are fairly comfortable.

These are the reasons why a trek to the Annapurna Sanctuary is considered suitable for beginners. However, even experienced trekkers will be equally satisfied, for who can resist approaching the first 8,000-metre peak ever to be climbed in mountaineering history. This feat occurred on 3 June 1950 when two French mountaineers, Maurice Herzog and Louis Lachenal, conquered Annapurna I.

Annapurna South and Hiunchuli, as seen near Dhampus.

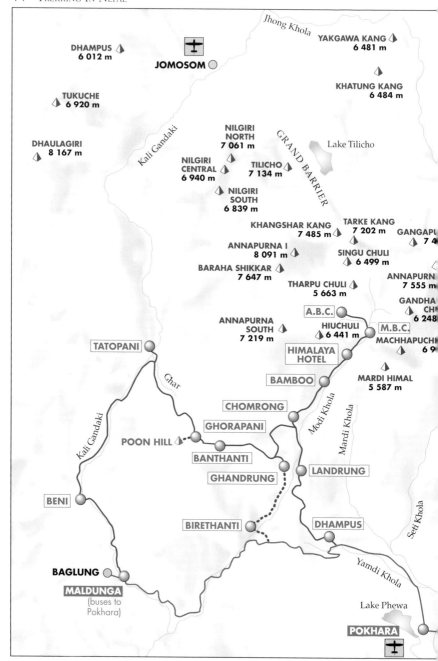

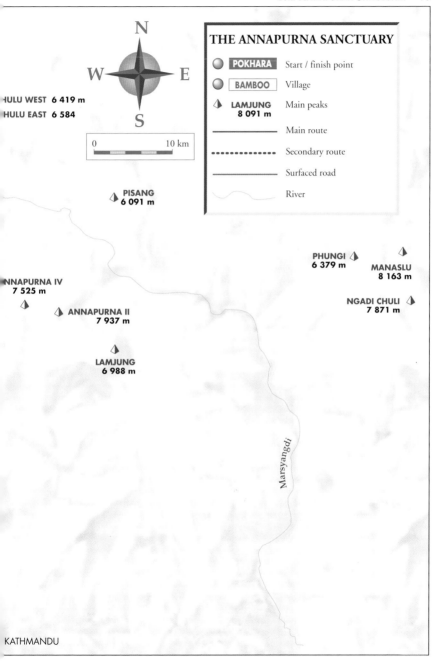

THE ANNAPURNA SANCTUARY

POKHARA   Start / finish point

BAMBOO   Village

LAMJUNG   Main peaks
8 091 m

———————   Main route

- - - - - - - - -   Secondary route

———————   Surfaced road

〰〰〰   River

N
W   E
S

0   10 km

HULU WEST 6 419 m
HULU EAST 6 584

PISANG
6 091 m

PHUNGI
6 379 m

MANASLU
8 163 m

NNAPURNA IV
7 525 m

NGADI CHULI
7 871 m

ANNAPURNA II
7 937 m

LAMJUNG
6 988 m

Marsyangdi

KATHMANDU

The First Day

FROM KATHMANDU TO POKHARA (Bus: about 8 hours)
Situated to the west of Kathmandu, Pokhara is Nepal's second largest town. Therefore, connections between the two cities are quite good. You can either fly or board one of the many tourist buses that leave every day.

About half a dozen public or private airlines are now competing for customers along this route as well but it is difficult to specify which one is currently the most efficient. You will have to find this out for yourself! Remember that the office of the Royal Nepal Airlines Corporation (RNAC) is located between Bir Hospital and the General Post-office (see map of Kathmandu, pages 18-19). The rate for a one way ticket is US$61 (to be paid for in US dollars unless you can show a currency exchange slip). The office of Nepal Airways is located on Kanti Path (see map of Kathmandu). It's probably simplest to have a travel agent fill you in on schedules and routes and handle your ticketing for you. There are several good agencies on Dubar Marg. During the off season it is possible to get special reductions in ticket prices. When you board the plane, try to get a seat on the right so you do not miss the incredible view of the Himalayan range (on your way back choose a seat on the left of the plane). The flight lasts about an hour.

The bus trip obviously takes longer - about seven hours. But it is much cheaper. Buy your ticket from any travel agent in Thamel. Make sure you book your seat at least one day before you plan to travel, and try to get a seat at the front of the bus. (The most spacious and less 'bumpy' seats are 1 and 2, side A.) Buses usually leave around seven in the morning from Kanti Path, opposite Grindlay's Bank (see map of Kathmandu). Stops are frequent and totally unpredictable. Buses usually stop for breakfast at about 9 am and again at around 12 noon for lunch at Mugling, a stopover village on the Prithvi Highway. Regarding highways, the Prithvi is a rather bad road which twists and turns for 206 kilometres along the banks of the Trisuli river. Landslides are common, especially during the monsoon. And every year, the road is manually rebuilt, stone by stone, creating regular traffic jams, or 'Nepali jams' as they are called. As a result, the length of the journey is uncertain.

For more information about this route, read Day 1 of the Around the Annapurnas itinerary (page 38) which gives detailed information of the road until Dumre. From here, the Prithvi Highway leaves the Marsyangdi Valley to join the Seti Khola Valley at Sankhar village. The bus then goes up the river for about 54 kilometres, before it reaches the bus terminal in Pokhara at Prithvi Chowk (see map, page 69).

Hotel and taxi touts will greet you as soon as you get off the bus. Even if these young men are annoying, they are not necessarily crooks. They are usually employed by a hotel who pays them a commission or baksheesh. Before you accept their services, make sure you agree on the prices, conditions and terms. Also always ask to see the room before you check in.

It would be tedious to draw up a list of all the lodges in Pokhara. Luxurious hotels stand cheek by jowl with shabby establishments.

The banks of Lake Phewa, in the Baidam area, are very popular among tourists. Among the most affordable hotels, we have already mentioned the Amrit Lodge (see page 71). We also recommend the Bahari Hotel (ex-Paradise Guest House), just behind the reputed Hungry Eyes Restaurant. Set amidst a flower garden, it offers about ten double bedrooms with private bathrooms, toilets and fans (very welcome in summer).

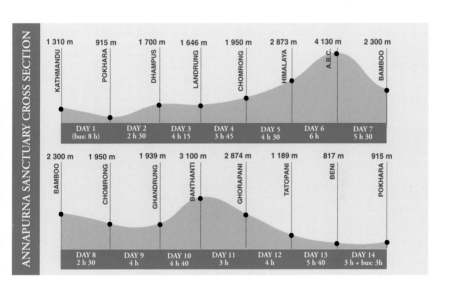

The Second Day

FROM POKHARA TO DHAMPUS (about 2 hours and 30 minutes)
For a long time, a trek to the Annapurna Sanctuary used to start from Pokhara
and involved a two day walk to reach the village of Dhampus. This was before
the arrival of four-wheeled vehicles. Till the eighties, trekkers had to endure
several hours of a bumpy jeep ride along the Yamdi Khola up to the camp at
Suikhet (1,100 metres), once a stopover for all the caravans coming down the
mountains with many stalls, small shops and tea and eating houses.

Today, there is a road from Pokhara to Baglung. A lodge was built instead of
wooden stalls. A handful of Tibetan refugees may still be trying to sell junk to
tourists arriving by taxi. The journey does not last for more than thirty minutes
and should not cost more than Rs150.

The beginning of the trek is still the same - the pathway cut into terribly steep
steps goes through a mixed forest. It takes about forty five minutes to reach the
Mina Lodge which marks both the end of this steep path and the arrival at
Dhampus, a large village spread over a vast plateau, 1,700 metres high. The
climb goes through fields and it is easy to miss the right trail. To ensure the right
direction, keep to the right. If in doubt, do not hesitate to ask the way at one of
the bhattis. From Mina Lodge to Dhampus Cold Drink should not take more
than thirty minutes. You will then find yourself in the middle of a forest once
again, but after forty five minutes of peaceful climbing you will reach the first
police checkpost at the entrance to Dhampus. During the last stretch of this day's
trek, you will have a magnificent view, from west to east, of Annapurna South
(7,219 metres), Hiunchuli (6,441 metres), Mardi Himal (5,587 metres), and to
the north, Machhapuchhare (6,993 metres). You will find the same view if you
check in at the Dhampus Lodge, a rather basic hotel, but very clean and quiet.
More discerning trekkers will choose the Basanta Hotel, five minutes before the
police station.

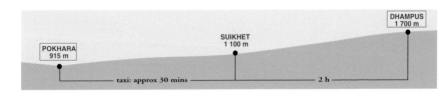

(Previous spread) A view of the Himalaya from Pokhara.

The Third Day

FROM DHAMPUS TO LANDRUNG (about 4 hours and 15 minutes)
After going down a fairly gentle slope cut into steps in the middle of the forest
for about an hour you will reach the village of Pothana, about 2,000 metres high.
You will find several lodges and restaurants here as well as the same magnificent
view as the previous day.

The path slowly ascends until it reaches the locality of Bhichok Deorali (2,149
metres). Deorali, sometimes spelt as Deurali, means a 'pass'. It takes about thirty
to forty five minutes to reach the top of this hill. At each crossing make sure you
keep to the right. As soon as you start going down you will find a few bhattis and
restaurants. Then the slope gets steeper until it meets the Modi Khola Valley first,
and then the village of Bheri Khola about thirty minutes away. Take a break and
have lunch here.

After crossing a small suspension bridge, the path follows the ridge of a hill
for about an hour until the first houses of Tolka (1,859 metres). It then crosses
the hamlets of Tolka Naga and Tolka Medi Gara, before going down again gently
to the village of Landrung (about an hour away). The forest now gives way to
vast expanses of terraced cultivations covering the surrounding hills.

Landrung (1,646 metres) is one of the first Gurung villages you will come
across. The Gurungs, about 180,000 people, represent the main ethnic group of
this middle range mountain region in central Nepal. Gurungs, together with the
Magars, form the mainstay of the Gurkha regiments in the British and Indian
armies. Originally from Tibet, they are mostly farmers though many have
adapted to modern tourism. Landrung is now a village where trekkers like to
stopover and there are several comfortable lodges offering international services
and menus. No comments!

For those in a hurry, please note that the last two days can easily be combined
as one.

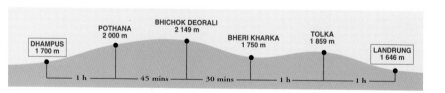

The Fourth Day

FROM LANDRUNG TO CHOMRONG (about 3 hours and 45 minutes)
At the junction after Landrung, the path which goes down steeply in the direction of the Modi Khola leads to Ghandrung, visible on the opposite side of the river. But you will have to walk towards the north on a path which gradually leads to the river's bank. It should take you forty five minutes to reach the locality of the New Bridge (about 1,500 metres).

After you have crossed the 'new' bridge - only about fifteen years old - the path rises rapidly and you will have a tough time, for about thirty to forty five minutes, before you can take it easy on a slope going down. You will then reach a small concrete bridge across the Kyumnu Khola, one of the tributaries of the Modi Khola, where there are some bhattis.

Climb the opposite slope for about thirty minutes until the hamlet of Jhinu Danda (1,760 metres) where there are a handful of lodges where you can stop for lunch. A forest path leaves the village and leads to some hot springs located on the banks of the Modi Khola. These are in fact two ponds, two metres by two metres each, made of concrete and supplied with hot water from the springs. Two changing rooms stand beside the ponds. The whole project was financed by a Malaysian association and is fairly popular with both the tourists and the local population. The water is continuously replenished and the ponds frequently cleaned which make them very pleasant to relax in or simply for a wash. You will have to return to Jhinu Danda afterwards. The return trip takes about an hour, excluding the time you spend in the bath.

The climb to Chomrong is a steep one. Expect an average slope rate of 30 percent. It will take you an hour to reach the hamlet of Taulung and from there another thirty to forty five minutes before you see the first houses of Chomrong. Fortunately, the route has a number of lodges which will make the necessary stopovers more enjoyable. Situated at about 1,950 metres, the Gurung village of Chomrong is one of the most important market towns of the area. It is built on the ridge of the Chomrong Khola Valley, exactly where this river meets the Modi Khola. The village controls the entry to the Sanctuary and offers the first clear views of Annapurna South, Hiunchuli and Machhapuchhare. The tourism industry has been beneficial to some of the inhabitants who have grown considerably richer and do not hesitate to demonstrate the fact. One evidence is the 60-metre-long paved stairway constructed by the successful landlord of the Himalaya Lodge. A signboard alongside thanks the benefactor for the donation of Rs20,000.

You will notice that the lodges in Chomrong look as grand as the best hotels in Pokhara. The most comfortable as well as the most expensive and the busiest ones are located in the upper part of the village. Affluent trekkers can also check into the now renowned Captain Lodge, in the lower part of the village, close to the cooperative managed by the Annapurna Conservation Area Project (ACAP). This lodge is run by an ex-noncommissioned Gurkha officer and offers about ten double bedrooms with hot showers (solar heated), as well as excellent international and Nepalese cuisine.

Terraced cultivations near Jhinu Danda.

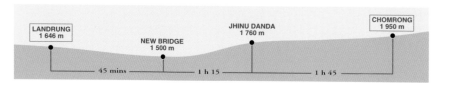

The Fifth Day

FROM CHOMRONG TO THE HIMALAYA HOTEL (about 4 hours and 30 minutes)
Go down until the suspension bridge which crosses the Chomrong Khola and
then climb up the opposite side for about thirty minutes till you reach the hamlet
of Banuwa. Carry on for another thirty minutes until you reach Sinuwa (about
2,400 metres) where you will find at least two lodge-restaurants. Here the path
leaves cultivated fields to enter a beautiful tropical forest. You can follow the
ridge of the hill, about 2,500 metres high, but unfortunately the mountain is
drained by several small streams and trekkers are forced to undertake a series of
ascents and descents. The climb is even more strenuous when it rains. It takes
about an hour to reach the locality of Khuldi Ghar (2,477 metres) where you will
encounter a second police checkpost. (You will have to show your trekking
permit as well as your entrance ticket to the National Park.) The headquarters of
the ACAP and its environmental centre are also located at Khuldi Ghar. (If
curious, inquire at the centre as to why you had to pay an entrance fee of Rs650
in Kathmandu. You will then learn more about their aims and objectives.)

After the checkpost, the path suddenly descends until it reaches the hamlet of
Bamboo (around 2,300 metres) where four or five lodges serve lunch.

As the name suggests, Bamboo marks the beginning of a huge bamboo forest
which leads, after about an hour of walking, to Tiptop (2,571 metres). There are
two lodges here competing with the lodges established in Doban (2,606 metres).
When the 'relocation' project undertaken by the ACAP commences, these lodges
will soon disappear, no great loss since neither are really worth it.

Soon after Doban, you will enter the sacred forest of Jode Yehm, where near a
waterfall on the east bank of the Modi Khola, you will see an altar surrounded by
thousands of white and red banners suspended from the trees. A sign indicates
the name of the place, and reminds travellers not to lean over. One assumes it is
better not to disturb the gods...

From Doban, it will take an hour to reach the Himalaya Hotel (2,873 metres).
There are other hotels available, probably the last comfortable ones of the trip.

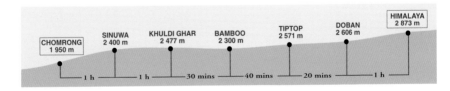

The Sixth Day

FROM THE HIMALAYA HOTEL TO THE SANCTUARY (about 6 hours)
The track continues through the middle of a forest, going up and down following the flow of the rivers, until the last stretch where a steep path leads to Hinku Cave (3,139 metres). It will then take another three hours to reach the actual site of Hinku Cave, noticeable by a huge rock half sheltering a bhatti. From here, it will take about thirty minutes to reach Deorali (three lodges, 3,230 metres). On the way, you probably would have crossed two neves, or slabs of old frozen ice, commonly found in glacial areas.

Walking from Deorali to Bagar (3,300 metres) takes about fifty minutes. Instead of lush vegetation, only bushes and high grasses survive. The path crosses the river twice on rather shaky bridges so as to avoid an avalanche and landslide prone area. You can have lunch in one of the two lodges in Bagar.

The next stop, the base camp of the Machhapuchhare, is about a two hour walk away. Machhapuchhare or 'fishtail', has been thus named because its twin summits resemble a notched fishtail. After you have walked along the river for thirty minutes, the path rises up again and goes through several neves. If it has snowed recently, this part of the route will be quite difficult, though the use of crampons will not be necessary, a stick should suffice.

At the MBC (Machhapuchhare Base Camp, 3,700 metres), you will find three or four tolerable lodges. Some trekkers like to stop here. However, if you want to enjoy the magnificent sunrise over the Sanctuary you may as well move on to the Annapurna Base Camp (ABC) which is only two hours away. Except for a few hills, the route is flat and therefore quite easy. Also, the spectacular views of Annapurna South, just before you, are so satisfying that you will easily forget your physical exhaustion. At the end of the route, at about 4,130 metres, you will find five or six lodges. A little further, the path leads to a small hill which is the best point from where to admire the entire panorama of the Sanctuary (see page 88 for details of the panorama).

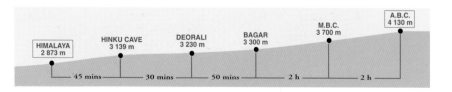

Days Seven And Eight

FROM THE ANNAPURNA SANCTUARY TO CHOMRONG

You have no other choice but to walk from the ABC to Chomrong. If you have the energy and weather permitting, you can walk from the Sanctuary to Chomrong at one stretch. However, expect to walk for at least eight hours. The worst part of the route is the climb from Bamboo to the checkpost at Khuldi Ghar. But the climb is effortless, mainly because the route is familiar and also because of the 'high' caused by the altitude. Nepalese porters can walk the entire distance in six hours. However, for those who prefer to take their own sweet time, it is best to cover the distance in two days and stay at Bamboo over night.

The return trip, and in fact the whole itinerary, may be disrupted in the future by the ACAP's 'relocation' project which plans to close down some stops, like Doban and Bagar, and to develop others, such as Tiptop. Indeed, there are far too many lodges along this route and it may be necessary to reduce the competition between them. Will tourists benefit is the question? Until now, trekkers can find a lodge almost every hour. Fewer stops also means less rest and perhaps more accidents. But let's wait until the project begins operations.

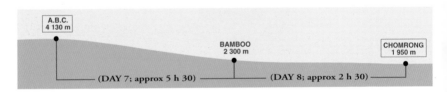

A.B.C.
4 130 m

BAMBOO
2 300 m

CHOMRONG
1 950 m

(DAY 7; approx 5 h 30) — (DAY 8; approx 2 h 30)

The Sanctuary's Panorama

You can see - to the south, Hiunchuli (6,441 metres) and Dakshin or Annapurna South (7,647 metres); to the northwest, Baraha Shikkar or Fang (7,647 metres) and Annapurna I (8,091 metres); to the north, Singu Chuli or Fluted Peak (6,499 metres), Tharpu Chuli or Tent Peak (5,663 metres) partly concealing Tarke Kang or Glacial Dome (7,202 metres) and Gangapurna (7,455 metres); to the northeast, the peak of Annapurna III (7,555 metres); to the east, Gandharva Chuli (6,248 metres) and finally, southeastwards, Machhapuchhare (6,993 metres).

(Previous spread) An avalanche on the slopes of Annapurna I.
(Right) Machhapuchhare and the ABC

The Ninth Day

FROM CHOMRONG TO GHANDRUNG (about 4 hours)

There are two options for the return trip to Ghandrung. For both, however, you have to start with a long, steep climb across Chomrong. About fifteen minutes after the village, and after bypassing the hill overlooking it, you will find a couple of bhattis just at the junction of two paths. There is a sign indicating the route, but it is easy to miss it.

The path which rapidly goes down in a southeastern direction leads to the hamlet of Jhinu Danda. This is your last chance to have a bath at the hot springs. Afterwards, take the path which leads to the New Bridge. After you have crossed a small bridge at the bottom of Jhinu Danda, climb the hill and make sure you don't miss the path on your right leading to Ghandrung. Arrows painted in black on the rocks should help you find your way.

After climbing for about thirty to forty five minutes, the path goes up and down the hills through the middle of a forest. Descend once more among terraced cultivations until you find a bridge across the Kyuri Khola, then climb to the opposite side. You will find more fields and it will take you another hour, with a difference of altitude of about 300 metres, to reach Ghandrung. Please note that you will only find a few isolated farms and no bhattis at all along this part of the route.

The second option is to take the path on your left at the junction which will lead you to the river and the village of Kyumnu Khola (1,750 metres) where you can stop for lunch.

After going up along the river, another steep path will take you to the hamlet of Kumrong built on top of a hill, 2,230 metres high. From here, the slope goes down until Ghandrung. The whole route takes about four to five hours.

Sitting at 1,939 metres, Ghandrung in one of the most important Gurung villages of the region. You will find many lodges here but the nicest ones are located in the upper part of the village. We recommend the Trekkers Inn or just next to it, Milan Lodge - both are new, quite comfortable and have a terrace overlooking Annapurna South, Hiunchuli and Machhapuchhare. Their rates are

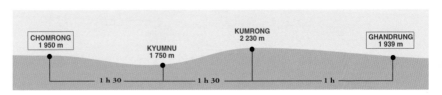

also quite reasonable. If you have time, you can pay a visit to the Gurung cultural centre nearby.

For those who would like to learn more about the traditional lifestyles of the people, it is best to walk around the village, perhaps visit a farm and drink some chang, the locally brewed beer made out of fermented corn. Another beverage you could sample is raksi, a rather strong alcoholic drink mixed with yak butter mixed with a handful of roasted rice, which can be drunk hot or cold.

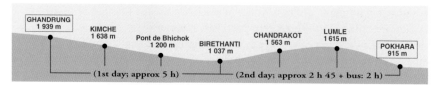

For Trekkers In A Hurry

For trekkers who may not have the time to go through Ghorapani and Tatopani, we have planned an alternative itinerary which enables them to reach Pokhara in two days.

From Ghandrung, walk in a southern direction to Kimche village (1,638 metres) where you can have lunch. From here, the path goes down, the difference in altitude is 400 metres, until the bridge at Bhichok. Keep walking along the west bank of the Modi Khola and follow the river until you reach Birethanti (1,037 metres), which is one of the stops for the Around the Annapurnas Trek (see pages 68 and 70). The route takes about four to five hours.

If you leave early enough in the morning, you can catch a bus or taxi back to Pokhara, a two-hour trip.

The Tenth Day

FROM GHANDRUNG TO BANTHANTI (about 4 hours and 40 minutes)
Reach the top of Ghandrung by heading towards the Hill Top Lodge or the Snow
View Hotel. After a government-run Tibetan carpet factory, the path enters a lush
tropical forest. A few minutes later you will reach Paradise Lodge, the last
habitation before the jungle. The path is easy going and after walking quite
comfortably for about an hour, you will reach the Kyunri Khola, one of the
tributaries of the Modi Khola, that you must cross on foot.

It will then take you about thirty to forty minutes to climb a path along a
small stream and reach the locality of Bhaisi Kharka (2,300 metres), which
means 'buffalo pastures'. You can stop for lunch at one of the two lodges here,
either the Hungry Lodge or the Hill Side Paradise Lodge. However, some
trekkers may prefer to carry on until Tada Pani where the selection is better.

It will only take forty five minutes of walking through a superb forest of giant
rhododendrons to reach Tada Pani or 'far from the water', situated at about 2,700
metres. You will find the path on your left, at the beginning of the village, close
to a volley-ball court, just between the Himalaya Lodge and Annapurna Lodge.

Walk through another forest until you reach a bridge across the Bhurungdi
Khola. The descent is quite steep and should take at least thirty minutes. The
next climb is also steep and should take an hour. You will then reach the Clean
View Lodge, the premier habitation in Banthanti, which, as its name suggests,
offers a clear view of the valley. The hamlet is about thirty minutes away,
squeezed between high cliffs at the base of a very humid valley.

Banthanti (3,100 metres), which means 'jungle shelter', is only partially
inhabited with about four or five lodges offering basic comfort and service. The
first, the Sun Rise Lodge, is about as good or bad as the others. You may decide
to stay overnight or continue, but you will definitely need to rest here since the
route to Ghorapani will take another three hours.

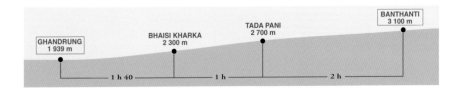

The Eleventh Day

FROM BANTHANTI TO GHORAPANI (about 3 hours)

It will take you an hour to reach Deorali from Banthanti. The path follows a small stream and you may have to make a series of ascents and descents because of landslides.

From Deurali (3,200 metres, two lodge-bhattis), you can climb right to the top of a hill called Gurung Tower, 30 minutes away, where the panorama resembles the one from Poon Hill in Ghorapani. Putali Himal, Mukut Himal, Dhaulagiri, Mount Tukuche, Nilgiris, Fang, Annapurna South, Hiunchuli and Machhapuchhare are all visible from here.

As you climb through the next forest of pine and rhododendron, views of Dhaulagiri improve. After a steep climb of fifteen minutes, the path becomes easier for about an hour and reaches a pass from where you can see the Kali Gandaki Valley to the northwest, and the Ulleri Valley to the southeast. It is here, just between Poon Hill and these valleys, that the airplanes connecting Jomosom with Pokhara go through. Lower down, you can see the village of Ghorapani (2,874 metres), which you will reach within the next forty five minutes.

Ghorapani, a very important stopover for the Around the Annapurnas Trek (see page 67), is still used by the many pony and donkey caravans that traverse the region. Hence, the meaning of Ghorapani — 'the watering place for horses'.

If you plan to climb Poon Hill, do so early the following morning so that you can enjoy the sunrise over the mountains. From the Hill Top View Lodge, situated at the highest point, Poon Hill is only an hour's climb away.

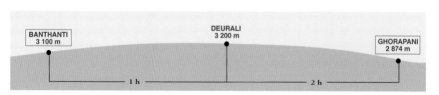

BANTHANTI
3 100 m

DEURALI
3 200 m

GHORAPANI
2 874 m

1 h   2 h

The Twelfth Day

FROM GHORAPANI TO TATOPANI (about 4 hours)
The origin of the name of Poon Hill, also spelt Pun Hill, comes from an ethnic sub-group of the Magars. This hill, 3,210 metres high, is famous for its panorama of the central Himalayan range. From its summit you can see, from west to east - Putali Himal (Butterfly Mountain), 7,246 metres; Mukut Himal (so called because it vaguely resembles a royal crown); Manapathi Himal (called after a local instrument of measurement), 6,380 metres; Dhaulagiri IV, 7,661 metres; Dhaulagiri I, 8,167 metres; Mount Tukuche, 6,920 metres; and Mount Dhampus, 6,012 metres. Then, on the other side of the valley, again from west to east - South Nilgiri, 6,839 metres; Baraha Shikkar (meaning 'twelve peaks'), 7,647 metres; Annapurna I, 8,091 metres; Annapurna South, 7,210 metres; Hiunchuli, 6,441 metres; Machhapuchhare, 6,993 metres; Annapurna IV, 7,525 metres; and finally Lamjung, 6,988 metres. To help you recover from both your excitement and the early morning departure, have tea or coffee at the Lovely Pun Hill Tea Shop. The panorama is so grand that you will overlook the exorbitant prices charged for a cup of tea.

The route between Tatopani and Ghorapani has already been described in the fourteenth day of the Around the Annapurnas Trek, page 67. Just keep in mind that the timings might be different.

Remember, it takes about thirty minutes to reach the village of Chitre (2,316 metres) and about an hour to reach the village of Shika (1,920 metres). You can climb up to Sika Deurali to have lunch. The walk from Shika to Ghara (1,768 metres) will take another hour. Soon after Ghara, the path rapidly goes down towards the Kali Gandaki Valley where it meets the Ghar Khola. This takes another hour. Two large suspension bridges cross both rivers. After you have crossed them walk along the west bank of the Kali Gandaki in a northern direction to reach the village of Tatopani, thirty minutes later.

Tatopani means 'hot water', a name derived from the nearby hot springs. Two pools have been formed by the river, slightly larger than the one at Jhinu Danda, but not as clean as both villagers and trekkers bathe here. An entrance fee is payable at a small hut, which also serves refreshments.

You will find several lodges in Tatopani. We recommend the Namaste Lodge.

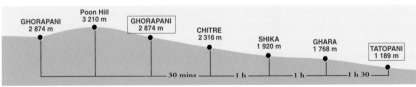

Dhaulagiri I and Mount Tukuche.
Annapurna South and Hiunchuli, seen from Poon Hill

The Thirteenth Day

FROM TATOPANI TO BENI (about 5 hours and 40 minutes)
Walk in a southern direction until you reach the two large bridges over the Kali Gandaki which you must have crossed the day before. Go across the river again,

A young girl from Ratopani.

but this time follow the eastern side until you reach the hamlet of Ratopani ('red waters'), about thirty minutes away. The path follows the bank of the river for another thirty minutes, until the river curves and forms a deep gorge. The path then goes up over a steep cliff before it abruptly descends towards the river where there is a suspension bridge surrounded by a few bhattis.

Keep to the east of the river and after an hour you will reach the village of Tiplyang (around 1,000 metres). Cross over a long suspension bridge to reach the west side of the Kali Gandaki. There are quite a few lodges/restaurants on the other side, where you can have lunch. Remember that there are very few places along this part of the route where you can find drinking water.

The distance between Tiplyang and Beni is about 14 kilometres. After a walk of about thirty minutes, you will reach the village of Begkhola or 'the fast river', so called because of the formation of rapids where the Beg Khola and the Kali Gandaki meet. Another thirty minutes away, is the village of Baishiri (several lodges), followed by the villages of Ranipauwa (one hour away) and Rahugat (872 metres), located at the confluence of the Kali Gandaki and the Gaulishor Khola. After Rahugat, the valley becomes wider and the route is almost flat. Beni (817 metres) is only forty minutes away and offers various types of accommodations.

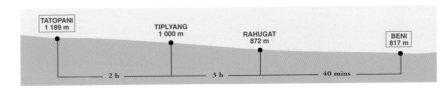

The Fourteenth Day

FROM BENI TO POKHARA (about 3 hours + 3 hours by bus)

To leave Beni, cross the iron bridge over the Kali Gandaki and follow the east bank for about two hours until you reach the village of Naglibang Phortse, after having crossed the hamlets of Patbeni, Diranbora and Salyang. The route is quite flat and plenty of water is available. It should be an easy walk unless it is a very hot and sunny day, then walking will be rather uncomfortable as there is not much shade at the bottom of the valley. Rest in Naglibang.

From here, it is only another hour before you reach Maldunga, also called the 'new bridge'. It is, in fact, a viaduct which enables one to cross the Kali Gandaki. The road which links Pokhara with Baglung also passes from here. There are various small stalls and bhattis which cater to both tourists and caravans coming down the mountains as this is the endpoint of the trek.

The Kali Gandaki, soon after Beni.

Buses, too, stop here to pick up passengers travelling to Pokhara which is about 60 kilometres away. The road goes through Kusma, then up along the Modi Khola before it takes the eastern direction and crosses Lumle, Nagdanda (your last police checkpost), Suikhet (the starting point of the trek) and finally Pokhara. Depending on the mode of transportation, the trip to Pokhara takes about three to four hours. The bus fare is Rs40. The fare on a Chinese pick-up is about Rs100. During the peak season you may get a chance to hire a taxi. Of course, the fares we mention here vary according to the season and are negotiable.

Once in Pokhara, make sure you buy your ticket back to Kathmandu the day before you plan to leave. Buses will drop you near the new Gongabu bus station, a fifteen-minute walk from Thamel.

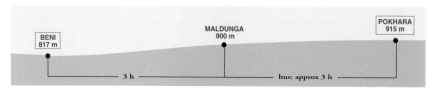

BENI
817 m

MALDUNGA
900 m

POKHARA
915 m

3 h   bus: approx 3 h

Gosain Kund, Langtang & Helambu

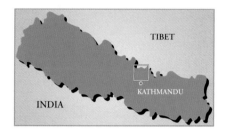

Introduction

The following sixteen-day itinerary is in fact a combination of three different shorter treks. It goes from the sacred Gosain Lakes to the rich valley of Helambu via the Langtang region, at the border with Tibet.

Lying at about 4,380 metres, the glacial Gosain Kund (kund means lake) is an important pilgrimage centre. Every year, during the monsoon, a festival takes place on full moon night attracting thousands of Hindus, both Nepalese and Indian, who come here to worship Shiva. According to legend, the waters of the lake were created when Shiva flung his trident onto the rocks. Then, this usually quiet place, with only a few lodges, is transformed into a hive of activity. Festivities take place everywhere and food and accommodation can be very expensive.

The narrow, high valley of Langtang, tucked in between Langtang Lirung (7,234 metres) to the north and a range of lower mountains (6,000 metres) to the south, attracts fewer pilgrims and trekkers. It is sparsely populated and access is difficult. Nevertheless, the region offers surprising contrasts. Up to 3,000 metres, the progression occurs along the Langtang Khola which runs through a narrow gorge, among several bamboo jungles and temperate forests. After Langtang village, where the National Park headquarters are located, the valley becomes wider and forests become alpine grasslands. Kyanjin Gyang or Kyanjin Gompa (3,950 metres), the last inhabited hamlet, serves as a summer pasture for yak herds. This is the closest you can get to the glacial area of the High Himalaya which forms the border with Chinese Tibet.

Shepherds' huts on the plateau of Keldang, with Ganjala Himal in the background.

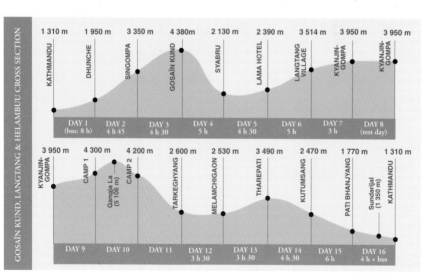

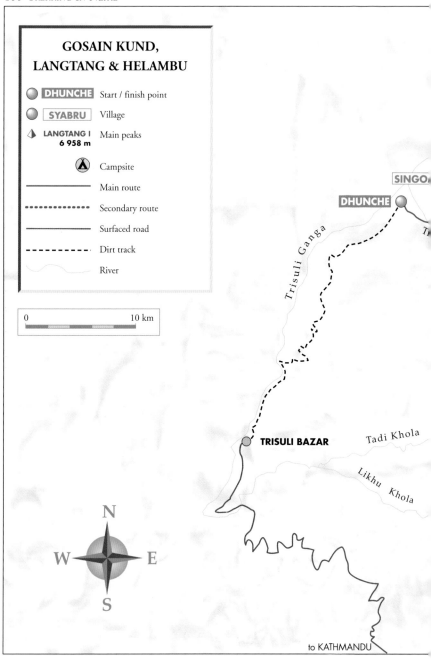

GOSAIN KUND, LANGTANG & HELAMBU

🔘 **DHUNCHE**	Start / finish point
🔘 **SYABRU**	Village
🔺 **LANGTANG I** **6 958 m**	Main peaks
🅰	Campsite
───────────	Main route
●●●●●●●●●●●●	Secondary route
───────────	Surfaced road
─ ─ ─ ─ ─ ─	Dirt track
∿∿∿∿∿	River

0   10 km

N
W   E
S

SINGO

DHUNCHE

Trisuli Ganga

TRISULI BAZAR

Tadi Khola

Likhu Khola

to KATHMANDU

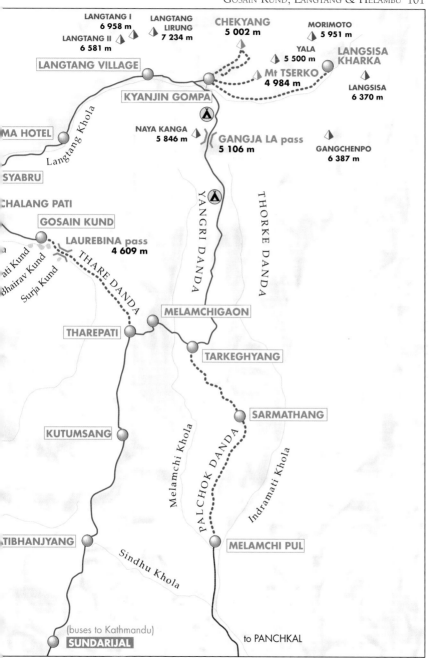

Lying 70 kilometres to the northeast of Kathmandu, Helambu, sometimes called Helmu, is celebrated for its picturesque villages, magnificent views and mild weather. The region is prosperous and hospitable and is mainly populated with Sherpas, distantly connected to the ethnic Sherpas found in the eastern region of Khumbu, around Everest.

The valley, drained by the Melamchi Khola, lies at a mid-range altitude and there are daily connections between the capital and the villages of Sundarijal and Panchkal. For these reasons, Helambu is a popular trek, especially among amateurs and trekkers in a hurry.

Indeed trekking to Gosain Kund, Langtang and Helambu is considered fairly simple, but only if they are undertaken separately.

Combining all three makes for a difficult and rather specialised trek. The crossing of the Gangja La (5,106 metres) specifically requires the services of a local guide. However, the following 'loop' itinerary can be divided into several 'mini' treks. The connections between them are described in the different sidebars. Here are some suggestions:

1) Gosain Kund only. The return trip takes six days with only four days of walking. (Read from day 1 to 3)

2) Gosain Kund to Langtang. This trek takes about fifteen days, which is rather long but since the average altitude hardly rises above 3,500 metres, there is no major difficulty. (Read from day 1 to 8).

3) Gosain Kund and Helambu. Requires about ten days. The only difficulty is crossing the Laurebina Pass (4,609 metres) which connects Gosain Kund to Helambu (see sidebar page 106). This is not a very high pass but it is easy to get lost especially if it snows. The services of a local guide is highly recommended. (Read from day 1 to 3 for Gosain Kund, and days 12 to 16 for Helambu).

4) Helambu only. Requires about eight days. To avoid taking the same route back, we suggest an alternative itinerary (see sidebar page 117) which will give you an opportunity to discover both sides of the valley.

The First Day

FROM KATHMANDU TO DHUNCHE (Bus : about 8 hours)
There is no 'tourist bus' connecting Kathmandu to Trisuli Bazaar, 71 kilometres away. Trisuli Bazaar is the entrance to the sacred lakes of Gosain and to the Langtang Valley. For a long time it was the starting point for all treks to these regions. A regular local bus to Dhunche, about 30 kilometres to the north, saves two days of a rather dreary walk (see sidebar below).

You can buy tickets from the new bus terminal in Gongabu (see map of Kathmandu, page 18–19). Daily departures are in the morning, at 7 and 7.30 am. It takes about four hours to reach Trisuli Bazaar (580 metres) where the bus usually stops for lunch. The ride is quite comfortable till this point. Later, the road becomes a dirt track with incessant twists and turns. This, combined with the hordes of passengers and poorly maintained vehicles, can turn the journey into a nightmare. Fortunately, the views of Trisuli Ganga below, that accompany the road for nearly four hours, are quite distracting. Please remember that just before you reach Dhunche, you will have to pay a fee of Rs650 to enter the Langtang National Park. Keep the receipt as you will have to show it again later.

Dhunche (1,950 metres), the main town of the Rasuwa district, lies where the Trisuli Khola - which originates in Gosain Kund - and the Trisuli Ganga meet. You will find many lodges here, though we recommend the Namaste Hotel or the Langtang View Hotel, both offering impeccable services and exceptional views of the Tibetan range and Mount Langtang, all for a very reasonable price.

For The Tough Trekkers

For those who prefer to walk, follow the catchwater drain from the Trisuli Bazaar hydroelectric plant up to a bridge which leads to the east bank of the Trisuli Ganga. The path runs along the motor track until Betrawati (625 metres), eight kilometres away from Trisuli Bazaar. At the end of the village, cross the Phalangu Khola and carry on until Ramche (1,700 metres), where you can stay overnight. After Ramche, you will have to cross the hamlets of Grang (1,850 metres) and Thare (2,000 metres). The path then joins the road and follows it until Dhunche.

The Second Day

FROM DHUNCHE TO SINGOMPA (about 4 hours and 45 minutes)
From Dhunche, take the road leading to Syabru Bensi to the northeast. At the end of the village there is a sharp U-turn, and a steep, narrow path starts on the right towards the direction of Gosain Kund. A yellow signpost with red arrows, installed by the Ministry of Tourism, indicates the right direction. You will see many of these signposts along the route.

Once you have crossed some fields, a forty five minute walk through brambles will take you to the banks of the Trisuli Khola. Cross the wooden bridge over the river where a water gauge shows the water level. There are camping sites on both sides of the river.

The path then slowly moves away from the north side of the river before it starts climbing up quite steeply in the direction of Deurali, which you should reach after two strenuous hours. Halfway through you will find a bhatti which occasionally serves food. The ascent continues through a rhododendron forest. After an hour, you will reach a crossroads where a signpost indicates that the path on the left leads to the village of Bhargu. The one on the right leads to the hamlet of Dhimsa (3,000 metres), a few minutes way.

Dhimsa is in fact a Nepalese army camp, and some of the bhattis close down during the off season. If so, carry on for about an hour until you reach the village of Singompa, perched on top of a ridge, 3,350 metres high.

At the dairy farm here, set up in association with a Swiss concern, you can purchase yak butter and yak cheese. You will also find two lodges, the Green Hill Hotel and the Evergreen Hotel and Lodge, where the rates are very reasonable. The Evergreen Hotel has a better location, however.

In the afternoon visit the chorten overlooking the village to the north. From here a path leads to a ridge that runs to the east and meets the main road to Singompa/Gosain Kund. If inclined, you can carry on through a marvellous forest of giant pine trees. The whole trip will take about two hours.

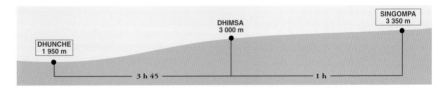

The Third Day

FROM SINGOMPA TO GOSAIN KUND (about 4 hours and 30 minutes)
After Singompa, the ascent is quite easy and only takes one hour to reach
Chalang Pati (3,584 metres) which has two bhattis-restaurants. The slope then
becomes steeper, and it takes at least an hour and a half of walking along the
ridge of a hill through stony scrubland to reach the hamlet of Laurebina, 3,900
metres high. Here, two lodges offer basic comfort (dormitory beds only). We
suggest that you have lunch here since this is the last inhabited spot before you
reach Gosain Kund.

Follow the ridge for another hour. The path then goes slowly downhill until it
reaches the first glacial lake, Saraswati Kund (around 4,000 metres). A little
further up, there is a second lake, Bhairav Kund (4,150 metres), and an hour
later, the final lake, Gosain Kund (4,380 metres), where thousands of Hindu
pilgrims congregate every year to worship Shiva.

In the small hamlet by the northern bank of the lake, among the many lodges
built for both trekkers and devotees, are several sanctuaries. Lodges offer a rather
rudimentary comfort with dormitory beds only. Be careful as many close down
during the off season.

In the afternoon, it is worth exploring the surroundings. There are some caves
which pilgrims use as shelters during the festival. A huge white rock, engraved
with a stylised trident, emerges dramatically from the centre of the lake. According to the legend, when the divine Shiva threw his trident (trishul in Hindi) here,
the glacier melted, giving birth to the Trisuli Khola.

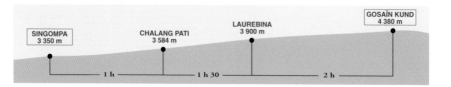

From Gosain Kund To Helambu Through The Laurebina Pass

The Laurebina Pass, at a height of 4,609 metres, is at a somewhat modest altitude for the Himalaya and presents no major technical difficulties. The track is quite clear and unless there is heavy snowfall, it is unlikely that you will get lost. However, since crossing a pass does entail some risk, we suggest that you use the services of a local guide. From Gosain, it is possible to reach Tharepati on the same day, although it would mean running rather than walking. Once again we suggest that you should plan to cover the distance in two days. When you leave the hamlet of Gosain Kund, walk along the northern bank of the river until you find the path leading to the pass. The climb may require about two to three hours, depending on your staying power. There are several smaller lakes along the way. The third one, called Surja Kund, is the largest as well as the closest to the track leading to the pass. The path suddenly descends along the northern bank of the Tadi Khola and it may take you about two hours to reach Ghopte where a few rocks will provide you with shelter for the night. Soon after Ghopte, there is a path which first ascends and then descends through a forest, until it reaches the village of Tharepati, described on the thirteenth day of the main itinerary.

The Fourth Day

FROM GOSAIN KUND TO SYABRU (about 5 hours)

There are two options to reach Syabru from Gosain Kund. The simplest, safest but also the longest one is to walk back until Singompa. After you have passed the dairy farm, you will find a crossroads. The path on the left leads to Dhunche; while the one on the right leads to Syabru, three hours away. It will therefore take about six to seven hours to cover the entire distance. To reduce the distance further, you can walk back to Chalang Pati, and then try to find, near the two bhattis mentioned on the second day, a yak trail going in a northern direction. This path, which goes through the middle of splendid forests of rhododendron and pine, is not clearly demarcated and is difficult to follow. Besides, it is quite steep and could be slippery if it has rained recently, so be extra careful. You will soon reach some pastures and fields in the middle of which the path suddenly disappears, or becomes a thousand too many. Keep to the north-north-west until you find the path coming from Singompa which will lead you to the village of Gardagaon (2,500 metres). The route to Syabru takes a maximum of five hours. This charming village adheres to the ridge of a hill, 2,130 metres high. This means that the difference of altitude for the day is about 2,250 metres. A fairly rough day for the leg muscles! Fortunately, there are many comfortable lodges, though we recommend either the Yeti Lodge or the Langtang View Lodge, both in the heart of the village.

The Fifth Day

FROM SYABRU TO THE LAMA HOTEL (about 4 hours and 30 minutes)
After the village, take the northeastern direction. You will find yourself amidst terraced cultivations and bamboo forests spreading across the banks of one of the tributaries of the Langtang Khola. A rather precarious bridge, close to a grain-mill, enables you to cross the river. You will find two bhattis on the other side. It takes slightly more than an hour to reach the southern bank of the Langtang Khola from Syabru.

Another two hours will take you to a suspension bridge across the river. The path is not really difficult but it goes up and down through a humid, subtropical forest. You may see monkeys in this dense jungle, but no other habitation except for the Bamboo Lodge, about half way through. However, we suggest you wait until the Namaste Tibetan Lodge, about forty five minutes later, to have lunch.

After the bridge, there is another landslide prone area and the ascent is pretty stiff until Rimche (2,440 metres), about an hour away. This hamlet offers two lodges and magnificent views of the Langtang Valley, with the village of Syabru in the background. A sign at a crossroads indicates the way to Sherpagaon. Ignore this path and carry on until the Lama Hotel, which is only thirty minutes away.

Set in the middle of a forest, this hamlet, 2,390 metres high, is a temporary one consisting of five or six lodges which cater to tourists. The oldest gives its name to the locality. However, our favourite is the Jungle View Hotel which offers individual beds with bamboo and curtain partitions.

The Sixth Day

FROM THE LAMA HOTEL TO LANGTANG VILLAGE (about 5 hours)
From the Lama Hotel, an hour's easy walk through the middle of a forest takes you to the Gumnachowk Lodge (2,690 metres). The valley then starts to widen, revealing the first views of Langtang Lirung, which is 7,234 metres at its highest point.

After one and a half hours, you will reach the hamlet of Ghora Tabela, which means 'the stables' (3,000 metres), where there are two lodges, a military camp and a police station, where you will have to show both your trekking permit and entrance ticket to the National Park.

Thirty minutes later, you will reach the Thangsyap Lodge (3,200 metres). The route is quite flat except for a steep climb in the last ten minutes. Then the path slowly climbs up to Langtang village (3,514 metres) which lies about two hours away.

You may come across a few huts along the way, closed for most of the time, and a small Tibetan village called Gumpa, about fifteen minutes before Langtang. At the entrance to the village you will see an army camp, the base of the Nepal's 11th Battalion. Remember that Chinese Tibet is not far away. Further away you can have a glimpse at the snowy slopes of Gangchenpo (6,387 metres)

Langtang is mostly populated by Tibetans, who are very hospitable. We recommend the, close to the health centre, where dormitory beds are available.

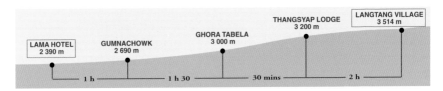

The Seventh Day

FROM LANGTANG VILLAGE TO KYANJIN GOMPA (about 3 hours)
During the winter season, when snowfalls are the heaviest, even Nepalese porters admit that it often takes them up to eight hours from Langtang village to reach Kyanjin Gompa - sometimes also called Kyangjin Gyang. However, under normal

conditions it should not take more than three hours, though it is advisable to take your time because mountain sickness could occur (see the chapter on Health, page 28) when you reach an altitude of 3,500 metres. Once you have passed the villages of Mund and Singdum, the path rises gradually until the Tajar Chu River. Cross a small wooden bridge. Though the gompa of Kyanjin is barely 30 minutes away, it is still not visible. However, you will be able to see the glaciers of Langtang.

Kyanjin, at an elevation of 3,950 metres, is mainly a summer pasture for yaks. Their milk is supplied to a small cheese factory nearby. You will also find five or six lodges, including the Yala Peak Lodge which offers individual beds in a large dormitory as well as a few bedrooms in a small separate building.

In the afternoon, the indefatigable trekker can explore Chekyang Peak which overlooks the village. It takes about two hours to reach its first peak at a height of 4,773 metres, covered with prayer flags. The path also leads to the second peak, 5,002 metres high, from where the view of the Langtang Lirung is absolutely splendid. You can also see Gangchenpo in the north, Naya Kanga (5,846 metres) in the southeast, as well as several other secondary peaks and glaciers.

The Eighth Day

AROUND KYANJIN GOMPA

To get acclimatised to the high altitude before the ascension of the Gangja La, we suggest that you spend another day around the gompa of Kyanjin Gompa. There are also several other excursions to choose from.

The best known one will lead you to Mount Tserko (4,984 metres). First climb the eastern side of the valley up to the hamlet of Chhongdu, then to the village of Yala. By following the ridge of the hill to the north of the village, you will reach the peak from where you have a panoramic view of the mountains - Langtang Lirung, Mount Yala (5,500 metres), Morimoto (5,951 metres), Langsisa Ri (6,370 metres), Gangchenpo (6,387 metres) as well as the Gangja La, to the south.

You can also follow the valley of the Langtang Khola further east up to Langsisa Kharka, where the river meets an impressive glacier. (Please note that jhang is the word for glacier in Nepalese.) This excursion will take the whole day so it may be a good idea to carry a picnic lunch.

Day Nine, Ten and Eleven

CROSSING THE GANGJA LA

Crossing the Gangja La (5,106 metres), which connects Langtang to Helambu, is considered very difficult and usually takes three days. We strongly advise you to hire a local guide who is familiar with the route. You can easily find one in Kyanjin Gompa. The minimum rate per day is Rs700, one way. Check and ensure that the guide you choose is experienced and owns proper equipment such as adequate shoes and sleeping bags.

It is not absolutely necessary to take a tent, though it may be useful if it snows or if you are reluctant to sleep out in the open.You should rent one in Kathmandu as you will not be able to find one elsewhere. It is very important to carry enough food and water as there are no habitations for the next three days. Also carry a portable stove instead of relying on wood fuel as trees are scarce at such a high altitude. Finally, if you are travelling during winter, a rope may be necessary to cross snow-covered ridges.

Apart from all these suggestions, crossing the Gangja La requires some experience of high mountains, and only expert trekkers should undertake it.

The first day
From Kyanjin Gompa, walk in a southern direction and cross the Lantang Khola via a corbelled bridge. After climbing for an hour through a rhododendron forest, you will reach an open plateau. Cross it diagonally until you reach a narrow steep slope which will lead you to another high plateau at an altitude of 4,300 metres. This is where you should spend the first night. If you have a tent you should be able to find a nice place to pitch it. If not, seek shelter under some rocks.

The second day
A long walk awaits you so make sure you start early, between 5 and 6 am the latest. Follow the Nasumkang Chu River until you can cross it. You then have to climb along the ridge of a hill for three hours until you reach the foot of the pass. Be careful as patches of snow cover the track here and there. The last part of the ascension leads to a corniced trail about 30 metres long. A thrilling experience!

Naya Kanga (5,846 metres), indicated as usual by several cairns and prayer flags, overlooks the pass. The descent might be quite perilous as the trail is scattered with big rocks and snow. For about an hour the path is indicated by small piles of rocks. The valley, drained by dozens of small rivers, widens and it becomes difficult to keep track of the path. It will take you between three and four hours to reach the plateau of Keldang, at a height of 4,200 metres. There are several shepherds' huts here where you can find shelter. This plateau dominates the valley of the Yangri Khola. In the background, towards the north, you can see the Kangjala Himal. On the opposite side, is the Thorke Danda range, to the west is the Yangri Danda range which blocks access to the basin of the Melamchi Khola.

The third day
The path, at an average altitude of 4,000 metres, is a series of ascents and descents until it reaches the Yangri Danda ridge. It follows the ridge until it descends abruptly, through a forest, and reaches Tarkeghyang. It feels like an endless day and many trekkers will be dead tired.

Sitting on a high plateau (around 2,000 metres) on the east bank of the Melamchi Khola, the village of Tarkeghyang, with its beautiful Sherpa houses and narrow streets, is very charming. The people are so warm and friendly that you will feel rejuvenated and the stress of the last three days will disappear. Do not miss the chance to visit the surrounding countryside, especially the gompa.

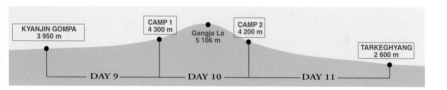

The Twelfth Day

F ROM T ARKEGHYANG TO M ELAMCHIGAON (about 3 hours and 30 minutes)
After descending for about an hour through terraced cultivations and forests, you will soon reach the hamlet of Nakotegaon on the east bank of Melamchi Khola. Cross the river over a suspension bridge. The altitude here is about 1,800 metres. Once on the other side, we suggest you take a tea break at the Riverside Lodge, as a further two or three hours' steep climb still awaits you before the village of Melamchigaon, perched on a plateau facing Tarkeghyang, at the height of 2,530

metres. The contrast between these two high plateaux is quite surprising. While Tarkeghyang appears compact, Melamchigaon is more spread out, with houses sprawled across the plateau. There are also several lodges. We particularly liked the Lama Lodge, close to the gompa. The chef prepares a delicious traditional sherpa soup with melted cheese, the taste of which is unusual, but if you drink it up, you will definitely please your hosts.

In the afternoon you can visit the monastery in the upper part of the village where it is said that Guru Rinpoche, one of the masters of Buddhism, once lived. It is located in an old cave engraved with sacred mantras (prayers). The sanctuary also has a beautiful image of the Guru which you should ask to see as it is not on view. There are other images of the Guru's disciples. The ceiling is painted with representations of the sun and the moon. There is also a small chapel which was once the monks' kitchen.

The gompa, in the centre of the village, is much more kitsch with a large, colourful collection of Buddhist images. Ask the owner of the Himalaya Lama Lodge to take you there. A small donation is always welcome.

Morning mist over Melamchigaon.
(Left) The Langtang Lirung glacier.

The Thirteenth Day

FROM MELAMCHIGAON TO THAREPATI (about 3 hours and 30 minutes)
When you are thirty minutes away from Melamchigaon, cross the bridge over one of the tributaries of the Melamchi Khola. The path is a steep climb in the direction of Thare Danda and it is a three to four hour walk over a nasty forest path to reach the hamlet of Tharepati.

The progress may be even more arduous if it rains, then the region is infested with leeches, which only adds to the discomfort.

At 3,490 metres, Tharepati is only a group of lodges offering basic comfort. The first one you will come across, the Top View Lodge, is no better or worse than the others. From a hill overlooking the village, you can have superb views of the Helambu Valley and Yangri Danda to the east, and of the Laurebina Pass towards the northeast. Try to get there early in the morning. Some say that if the weather is clear, you can even see Kathmandu.

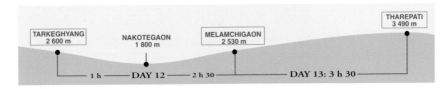

The Fourteenth Day

FROM THAREPATI TO KUTUMSANG (about 4 hours and 30 minutes)
An easy day which starts with an hour's walk through a rhododendron and oak forest until you reach the village of Magen Goth (3,150 metres) where a couple of bhattis await you. Then, the path goes down, sometimes quite steeply, and sometimes along a scree covered slope. This lasts for about three hours until you

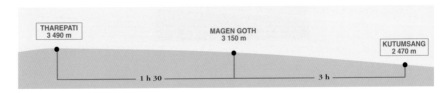

reach Kutumsang (2,470 metres). On the way you will find a few lodges and bhattis, some closed, some open.

At the beginning of the village is the National Park Office where you must have both your trekking permit and your entrance ticket checked. If you have lost the latter, you are liable to pay a fine of Rs2,000. Except for its beautiful scenery, Kutumsang has nothing much to offer. Even its lodges are all more or less the same.

The Fifteenth Day

From Kutumsang to Patibhanjyang (about 6 hours)

The descent from Kutumsang to the village of Gul Bhanjyang (2,130 metres) goes through a pleasant forest and takes about an hour and a half. You have to walk for another thirty minutes along the ridge of a hill to reach the hamlet of Bettini first and then the point marked 2,521 metres. From here you must start going down a rocky path towards Chipling (2,170 metres). By now, you would have walked for four hours so it may be a good idea to stop for lunch.

Thirty minutes after you leave Chipling, the descent eases and you will find yourself in the middle of the fields, at an altitude of about 2,000 metres. The walk to Patibhanjyang, which sits atop a small hill at 1,770 metres, takes an hour and a half. You will have the choice between several lodges, the largest being the Pati Lodge, in the heart of the village.

The Sixteenth Day

From Patibhanjyang to Kathmandu (about 4 hours + bus)

Climb up for about an hour until the hamlet of Chosa Pani where you will find several lodges and bhattis. From the point marked 2,141 metres, views of the Likhu Khola Valley on the west, the Talamarang Khola Valley towards the northeast, and the Sindhu Khola towards the southeast, are absolutely splendid.

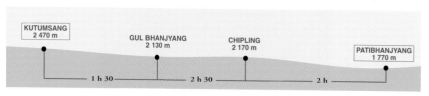

Soon after Chosa Pani, the track which leads to Sundarijal improves enough for motor vehicles to drive on. If you want to avoid it take a narrow path going through a lush tropical forest. However, this path has earned a bad reputation as several trekkers have been attacked by armed bandits. In order to avoid getting lost or being ripped off, it is best to join one of the many caravans going daily to Sundarijal.

From Chosa Pani, it takes about two hours to reach the rather ugly village of Mulkharka (1,895 metres); and another hour of descent to reach the reservoir supplying water to Kathmandu. The catchwater drain will take you directly to Sundarijal (1,350 metres).

This small market town is 11 kilometres away from Kathmandu. There are regular mini-buses but taxis can also take you directly to your hotel.

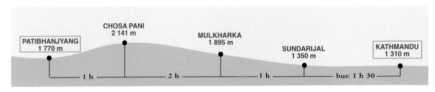

Menu at the entrance of a lodge.

The Two Sides Of Helambu

For those who can only spend one week in Helambu, here is an itinerary which enables them to take a different route on their way back. The departure town is still Sundarijal, which you can reach by bus from Kathmandu. The first five days correspond to days 12 to 16 of the main itinerary, to be read in the reverse order.

On the sixth day, take the path leading to the Sherpa village of Sarmathang (2,664 metres), through Gangjawal. The walk takes about three and a half hours. On the seventh day, follow the ridge of the Palchok Danda which goes between the basin of the Indrawati Khola towards the east, and the Melamchi Khola towards the west. After five or six hours, you will reach the large village of Melamchi Pul, 890 metres. It will then take you two hours by mini-bus to reach Panchkal, 30 kilometres away. From here you can catch another bus which, via the Arniko Highway, connects daily to the capital.

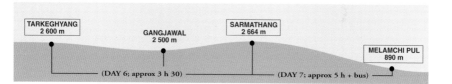

TARKEGHYANG
2 600 m

GANGJAWAL
2 500 m

SARMATHANG
2 664 m

MELAMCHI PUL
890 m

(DAY 6; approx 3 h 30) ———— (DAY 7; approx 5 h + bus)

From Jiri To Namche Bazaar

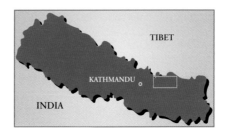

Introduction

On 10 March 1953, a team of 12 mountaineers from New Zealand and Britain, led by General Sir John Hunt, are preparing to climb Mount Everest from Bhadgaon, only 20 kilometres away from Kathmandu. With them are nearly 400 Nepalese porters, recruited to carry eight tonnes of material and equipment. The endless climb slowly begins as the sun rises. Hundreds of curious Nepalese have come to watch, with disbelief, the 'white foreigners' who claim they can conquer and hoist their flag on top of Chomolungma, the 'Mother Goddess', more commonly called Everest, the highest mountain in the world. It took this unusual caravan more than fifteen days to reach Namche Bazar, in the high mountain region of Khumbu. The rest of the story is now a legend. On 29 May, at 11.30 am, Tibetan, Tenzin Norgay and New Zealander, Edmund Hillary, were the only two men to reach the summit, the first time anyone had ever climbed the Roof of the World.

The following itinerary invites you to follow in the tracks of these pioneers. Much has changed over the last 44 years, the most important of which is the road between Kathmandu and Jiri via Lamosangu, which has reduced the older 1953 route by several days.

For the first six days, the path goes across a hilly region, with an average altitude between 2,500 and 3,000 metres, where terraced cultivations dominate. What may seem as an easy walk is in fact not, as the local irrigation system creates complications. The area is irrigated by two tributaries of the Sun Kosi - the Khimti Khola and the Likhu Khola - which flow from the north to the south,

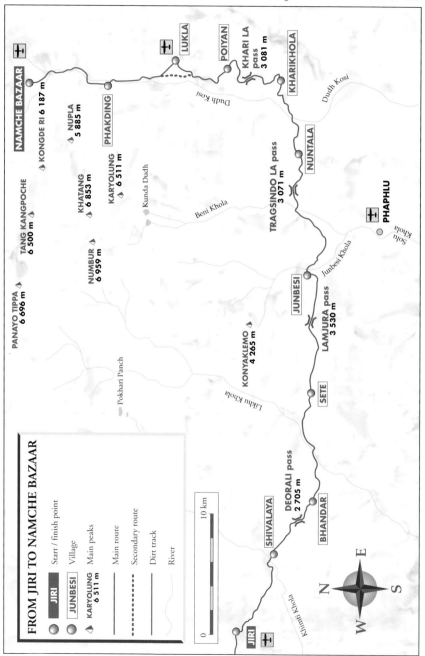

FROM JIRI TO NAMCHE BAZAAR

- JIRI — Start / finish point
- JUNBESI — Village
- ◬ KARYOLUNG 6 511 m — Main peaks
- —— Main route
- ·········· Secondary route
- —— Dirt track
- —— River

0 — 10 km

NAMCHE BAZAAR
◬ KONGDE RI 6 187 m
TANG KANGPOCHE 6 500 m ◬
PANAYO TIPPA 6 696 m ◬
NUMBUR 6 959 m ◬
KHATANG 6 853 m ◬
KARYOLUNG 6 511 m ◬
NUPLA 5 885 m ◬
PHAKDING
LUKLA
POIYAN
KHARI LA pass 3 081 m
KHARIKHOLA
Dudh Kosi
Dudh Kosi
NUNTALA
Kunda Dudh
Beni Khola
TRAGSINDO LA pass 3 071 m
PHAPHLU
Solu Khola
JUNBESI
Junbesi Khola
LAMJURA pass 3 530 m
KONYAKLEMO 4 265 m ◬
Likhu Khola
Pokhari Panch
SETE
DEORALI pass 2 705 m
SHIVALAYA
BHANDAR
JIRI
Khimti Khola
N
E
S
W

The Buddha from Junbesi Temple.

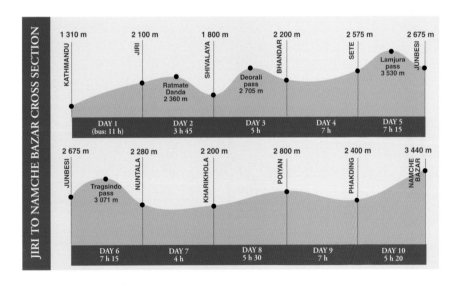

JIRI TO NAMCHE BAZAR CROSS SECTION

1 310 m	2 100 m	1 800 m	2 200 m	2 575 m	2 675 m
KATHMANDU	JIRI	SHIVALAYA	BHANDAR	SETE	JUNBESI

Ratmate Danda 2 360 m

Deorali pass 2 705 m

Lamjura pass 3 530 m

DAY 1 (bus: 11 h)	DAY 2 3 h 45	DAY 3 5 h	DAY 4 7 h	DAY 5 7 h 15

2 675 m	2 280 m	2 200 m	2 800 m	2 400 m	3 440 m
JUNBESI	NUNTALA	KHARIKHOLA	POIYAN	PHAKDING	NAMCHE BAZAR

Tragsindo pass 3 071 m

DAY 6 7 h 15	DAY 7 4 h	DAY 8 5 h 30	DAY 9 7 h	DAY 10 5 h 20

while the route goes from the west to the east. This means that you have to go across terrain riddled by rivers, and cross at least one pass almost every day.

After Nuntala, the path meets the Dudh Kosi Valley and takes a northward direction until Namche. Both the countryside and the people change, as you enter the homeland of the Sherpas, a people who occupy a special place in the history of mountaineering.

As for the celebrated peaks, except for a glimpse here and there, they can hardly be seen yet, making this part of the route, called the 'approaching walk', a truly magical one.

The First Day

From Kathmandu to Jiri (bus: about 11 hours)

Direct bus services connect Kathmandu with Jiri, in the Dolakha district. You can buy tickets from the Durbar Marg bus station (see map of Kathmandu, pages 18-19). Buses depart daily at 5.30 am, 6.30 am and 7.30 am. If you decide to take the first bus, you can book your seat the day before. For the later buses, you will need to buy your ticket at least an hour before departure. Although bus seats are meant for two, local travellers use the space to accommodate three or even four people. If you want to make your trip more comfortable and less of a nightmare, we suggest that you buy one extra ticket per person. Don't forget that you are going to spend more than eleven hours on this bus.

The distance between Kathmandu and Jiri is about 180 kilometres. For the first 78 kilometres, the bus drives along the Arniko Highway, built with the help of the Chinese government, which leads on to Tibet. After Kathmandu, you will cross Bhadgaon, Banepa, Dhulikhel, Panchkal and Dolalghat. Dolalghat, where the Indrawati and the Sun Kosi meet, is a paradise for river rafting. The road then follows the Sun Kosi River in a northern direction until the hamlet of Khadi Chaur, about 30 kilometres away from Lamosangu, where it crosses the river over a large steel bridge.

The bus then leaves the Arniko Highway to follow the ridge of a hill until the

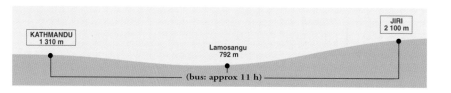

KATHMANDU 1 310 m — Lamosangu 792 m — JIRI 2 100 m

(bus: approx 11 h)

village of Muldi where it usually halts for lunch. By this time you would have already travelled for six hours. An hour and a half later, the bus reaches Charikot Bazar, followed by Kirantichhap and Tamba Kosi. It then wends its way through the villages of Namdu and Maina Pokhari. After the Hanumante Pass, the road descends towards Jiri (2,100 metres), an important centre of trade and the departure point for Khumbu, hence the number of lodges you find here. The most acceptable is the Sagarmatha Guide & Restaurant Lodge, in the centre of the village.

The Second Day

FROM JIRI TO SHIVALAYA (about 3 hours and 45 minutes)

After the small bridge in the middle of Jiri, which marks the end of the road, take the path on your right to climb through the midst of a beautiful pine forest. Fifteen minutes later, you should be overlooking the hospital compound. It will

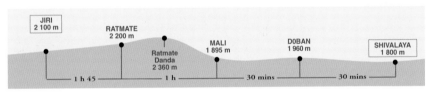

then take you thirty minutes to reach the hamlet of Bagh Khor. Though Bagh Khor means 'tiger place', all the big cats have disappeared. The area is fairly domesticated now and mainly confined to terraced cultivation.

Follow the path for an hour until you reach the hamlet of Ratmate, 2,200 metres high, where there are several lodges. Climb for another fifteen minutes to find the bhattis at Ratmate Danda, just before a flat area about 2,360 metres high, from where you have a beautiful perspective of the Rolwaling Himal range. This is the beginning of a long descent (about forty five minutes), towards the village of Mali (2,200 metres), where you can stop for lunch. Later, the path continues to go down towards the hamlet of Doban (1,960 metres) and the banks of the Yelung Khola. This part of the route, through rhododendron forests, is very enjoyable. Cross the river over an old wooden bridge and follow the north side of the Yelung Khola until it meets the Khimti Khola at Shivalaya (1,800 metres high), named after the Hindu god, Shiva. About half of the twenty houses in the village have been turned into lodges. The cheapest and the one offering the best dal bhat is the Shivalaya Lodge & Restaurant, right at the beginning of the village. To end this rather short day, take a walk to Those, along the Khimti Khola.

The Third Day

FROM SHIVALAYA TO BHANDAR (about 5 hours)

After the first bridge at the beginning of Shivalaya, you will find a police checkpost which also marks the border between the districts of Dolakha and Ramechhap. To have one's trekking permit checked here is a mere formality as the police are quite unconcerned.

At the end of the village, you have to cross a second bridge which leads to a narrow, steep path which in turn climbs among terraced cultivations and enters a pine forest. It will take you an hour to reach the village of Sangbadanda (2,200 metres), with its few bhattis, spread across an open area.

From here, though the slope becomes gentler, the climb is still tough and it will take you about two to three hours to reach the 2,705 metre high Deorali Pass.

The only two villages you will come across are those of Khasrubas and Ghalta Ghar. The latter has several lodges where most trekkers stop for lunch. The slope becomes steep again until the pass.

The hamlet of Deorali is of little interest except for a view of the gigantic high altitude plateau of Bhandar, some 500 metres below. You can also buy yak cheese and curds made in the nearby village of Thodung, famous for its dairy farm and gompa.

The climb down from Deorali takes at least an hour. The path down is cut into a flight of steps which makes the descent very tiring. After some cultivated fields, the slope becomes gentle again, but it will still take forty five minutes to reach the first habitation of Bhandar (2,200 metres). Prayer flags and chortens atop the village's public square inform visitors that they are entering a Buddhist region.

If you circumambulate the chortens (do so from the left as is the custom based on the direction the earth rotates), you will enter a grassy area where Bhandar's most luxurious lodge, the Ang Dawa Lodge, is situated. If you want a family-type lodge, the Sherpa Lodge at the entrance of the village, is suitable.

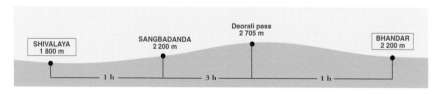

The Fourth Day

From Bhandar to Sete (about 7 hours)

From Bhandar, go down the plateau towards the village of Dokarpa (about 2,000 metres), forty five minutes away. Cross the Thado Khola over a charming wooden bridge and turn immediately to the left. After a few minutes' walk along the ridge of a hill, the path suddenly descends through a rhododendron forest towards the Surma Khola Valley. If you are travelling during the month of March, the trees will be covered with flowers.

It takes about an hour to reach another bridge surrounded by bhattis. If you follow the northern bank of the Surma Khola, you will soon reach the place where it meets the Likhu Khola. Follow the west bank of the latter until Pekarnasa (about 1,550 metres), about an hour away.

Walk on its east side this time, and follow it for an hour until Kenja (1,600 metres), a very beautiful village perfect for lunch. Your trekking permit will be checked again soon after the suspension bridge over the Kenja Khola.

To reach Sete from Kenja will take three and a half hours. This does not take into account the necessary rests you will have to take now and then. This is probably the first tough day of the trek as the slope is terribly steep with an altitude difference of about 1,000 metres.

Set at an elevation of 2,575 metres, on top of a narrow high plateau, the village of Sete only offers basic accommodation so we can only recommend the Dreamland Lodge & Restaurant.

The Fifth Day

FROM SETE TO JUNBESI (about 7 hours and 15 minutes)
When you leave Sete, you will find that the path rises rapidly to reach the top of the hill. It will take you an hour to reach the hamlet of Dagchu (around 3,000 metres). From the upper part of the village, you can see Mount Konyaklemo (4,265 metres). After Dagchu, a short descent will lead you to an open, flat area with a pond where buffaloes come to drink and bathe. From here take the path on your left and follow it until you reach the Lamjura Pass. Thereafter, cross the villages of Kathbisaune (an hour away) and Goyem (thirty minutes away) where you can have lunch.

After Goyem, a forty five-minute walk through a beautiful forest will take you to the next bhattis. The vegetation then becomes more scarce and the path slowly ascends until it reaches an open, flat area surrounded by a mani wall. From here you will see the entire Kenja Khola Valley towards the south, and Likhu Chuli (6,718 metres), Panayo Tippa (6,696 metres), Numbur (6,959 metres) and Karyolung (6,511 metres) towards the north. It will take another hour to reach the pass. For the first thirty minutes, the path easily follows the ridge of the hill (this may be more difficult during the winter). Midway, you will find a handful of lodges situated in a denuded area. Then the path climbs up steadily until the Lamjura Pass (3,530 metres), indicated as usual by the ubiquitous chortens, mani walls and prayer flags. It is now time to go down towards the Tragdobuk Khola Valley.

After forty five minutes of walking across a steep slope in the middle of pine trees, you will find two forest bungalows, now used as bhattis. The slope is quite gentle when you enter the hamlet of Taktur. Carry on until you reach the village of Tragdobuk (2,860 metres), about an hour and a half away from the Lamjura Pass. Climb the northern slope to avoid a hill. When you see the narrow path leading down to the village of Phaphlu, you will know that you are approaching Junbesi (2,675 metres), only thirty minutes away. This small and prosperous market town has all the facilities trekkers require, including a post-office. You can visit the local gompa as well as the region's largest chorten. There are several lodges, of which we recommend the Junbesi Lodge.

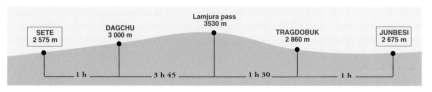

The Sixth Day

FROM JUNBESI TO NUNTALA (about 7 hours and 15 minutes)
Soon after you reach the chorten at Junbesi, cross the Junbesi Khola and climb
the path going up through a pine forest. The climb is pretty tough for about an
hour, but it becomes easier soon after you leave the forest, although it will still
take you another hour to reach the village of Purtyang Beni. From the terrace of
the Sherpa View Lodge, you will finally survey from left to right the first grand,
all-embracing vista of the route - Everest (8,848 metres), although only a mere
glimpse of the peak, Tramserku (6,608 metres), Kang Tega (6,685 metres),
Kusum Kangguru (6,369 metres) and Mera (6,476 metres).

From here, a long walk along the ridge of a hill will take you to the village of
Solung (2,984 metres) where you should stop for lunch before you start descending towards the Beni Khola (2,550 metres), an hour's walk away. Cross the
river over a suspension bridge that leads directly to the village of Ringmo (2,800
metres). Walking amidst another pine forest from Ringmo to the bhattis of
Pangoma takes about forty five minutes. The slope is a bit stiff but do not
despair, the Tragsindo La, at 3,071 metres, is only thirty minutes away.

The village of Nuntala (2,280 metres) is still two hours away. Nun in Nepali
means 'salt', hence the village's name, derived from its former position as a major
centre of trade. The trading of salt has slowly declined and has now been replaced by tourism. All the lodges here offer a good price/quality ratio.

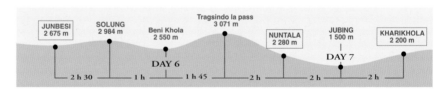

The Seventh Day

FROM NUNTALA TO KHARIKHOLA (about 4 hours)
It takes two hours from Nuntala to reach the banks of the Dudh Kosi, also called
the 'milky river', which has its source in the region of the Gokyo Lakes (see page
148). For the first thirty minutes, or until the hamlet of Phuleli (about 2,100
metres), the slope is quite steep. Then it becomes gentler but it is still a long, one

hour walk along the ridge of the hill before you start the descent towards the bottom of the valley.

Near the suspension bridge, that enables you to cross over to the east side of the river, there are several bhattis which indicate that you are near the Rai village of Jubing (1,500 metres high). In spite of the presence of a few lodges, signifying the timid entry of modernisation, these people lead a very traditional lifestyle. Another reason why you should stop here for lunch.

From Jubing to Kharikhola, the path goes up amidst fields of corn, wheat or potato, depending upon the season. After an hour and a half, the path goes around a huge hill, behind which nestles the village of Kharikhola (2,200 metres). The centre of the village, indicated by a chorten, is still thirty minutes away. The village is used as a stopover by all the travel agencies organising treks to this region so independent trekkers, in order to avoid the crowds, may prefer to continue walking until the hamlet of Bupsa, two hours away.

The Eighth Day

FROM KHARIKHOLA TO POIYAN (about 5 hours and 30 minutes)

The alternate route to Poyan via Bupsa, is an easy though long walk. It goes over the hill overlooking Kharikhola. If you choose this option, cross the bridge over the Khari Khola and climb until you reach Kharte (2,683 metres), one and a half hours away. Stop and have lunch here as there are only indifferent places ahead.

After Kharte, the path continues upwards, this time amidst a tropical forest. If you trek during the spring, you will see beautiful magnolias in bloom. The jungle route, 2,800 metres high, lasts for about an hour and goes up and down, crossing several rivers. After Kare, where there are only two mediocre bhattis, it is only another hour before you reach the Khari La (3,081 metres).

Going down to Poiyan is an easy job. For the next two hours the path follows a bamboo forest until it reaches this small hamlet (2,800 metres), with its two small, fairly pleasant lodges.

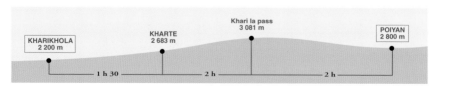

The Ninth Day

From Poiyan to Phakding (about 7 hours)

It takes two hours to reach Surke from Poyan. The first half of the route goes along a hill until Chutok La (2,945 metres) where there are a few bhattis. Afterwards, you have to climb down 500 metres or so until you reach the Surke bridge.

At the end of Surke, there is a mani wall which conceals a crossing so be careful you do not lose your way. The main itinerary follows the 2,400 metre altitude line, overlooking the Dudh Kosi. Trekkers who have chosen to walk back to Jiri should carry on straight ahead until Phakding, four hours away.

Others should follow the path on their right towards Lukla, a two-hour climb away. This loop is necessary if you want to book your return ticket to Kathmandu. Perched on a plateau, 2,800 metres high, the village of Lukla has a small airport with daily connections to the capital (also see the introduction to the Everest Base Camp Trek, page 130). The offices of the various airlines flying from Lukla to Kathmandu are located in the centre of the village. Hours vary but they are always open between 3 and 5 pm. The fare for a one way ticket is US$83, payable by cash if you are carrying US dollars, or by travellers' cheques if you show your passport. Make sure you understand when and how to have your ticket reconfirmed since it is always a complicated process.

Walking from Lukla to Phakding takes three hours. Going in a northern direction, you first cross the village of Choplung (forty minutes), then the village of Tado Khola (another forty minutes away) which offers a nice view of the Kusum Kangguru (6,369 metres) towards the east. After the river, a short but steep slope leads to Ghat (2,600 metres). At the end of the village, you will see several large rocks and a small chorten, where you will have to start the descent towards Phakding (2,400 metres), less than an hour away. Carry on in the direction of a large suspension bridge across the Dudh Kosi. On the west bank, two shelters, the Sun Rise Lodge and the Five Stars Hotel, are quieter than the hotels in the centre of the village.

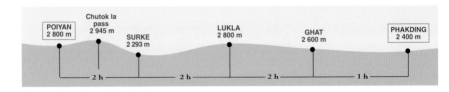

The Tenth Day

FROM PHAKDING TO NAMCHE BAZAAR (about 5 hours and 20 minutes)
The path first rises steeply, then follows the hill overlooking the west bank of the Dudh Kosi. It takes thirty minutes to reach the hamlet of Zanfute, where you will find a few bhattis set in the middle of a beautiful pine forest.

After crossing a small bridge, the path continues until a small lodge called the Himalayan Lodge. This is where you will start the climb towards the village of Bemkar, about 2,800 metres high. For about forty minutes, you will have to undertake a chaotic trek comprised of a series of ascents and descents in the middle of the forest, followed by a stretch of rock climbing. It is imperative that you concentrate as the glimpses of the impressive east slope of Tramserku (6,608 metres) can be quite distracting.

From Bemkar, it hardly takes ten minutes to reach an old and not very strong wooden bridge crossing over the Dudh Kosi. By following the eastern side of the river, you will soon reach (within thirty minutes) Chumoa. This village has several lodges, especially the Hatago Lodge which looks like a ranch and is famous for its peach wine. Walk for another twenty minutes to reach the market town of Monjo (around 2,800 metres). Cross the bridge over the Kyashar Khola, to reach, ten minutes later, the army camp of Jorsale, which is also the entrance to the Sagarmatha National Park. Sagarmatha is the Nepalese name for Everest. You will have to show both your trekking permit and entrance ticket to the National Park.

The village of Jorsale is only another ten minutes away from the checkpost. Cross the bridge over the Dudh Kosi and you will find several restaurants where you can stop for lunch.

At the end of the village there is a corbelled bridge which leads to the east bank in the centre of a forest, which again leads to another bridge - the last one for the day! The two hour ascension to Namche is quite tough. Halfway through, there is a bhatti, called the Everest View Tea Shop, where you can stop and rest.

Namche Bazar, the commercial centre of Khumbu, at an altitude of 3,440 metres, sits in the middle of a cirque. See page 134 for details of the facilities it offers.

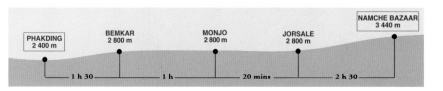

Everest Base Camp

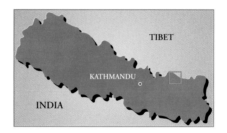

TIBET

KATHMANDU

INDIA

Introduction

The trek to Everest Base Camp leads to the summit of Kala Pattar (5,545 metres), the highest point you can reach in the Nepalese Himalayan range. From the top you have the best view of the surrounding giant peaks. Because of the extremely high altitude and the rough weather conditions, it is also the toughest trek of the whole range. Beginners should think twice before they undertake it.

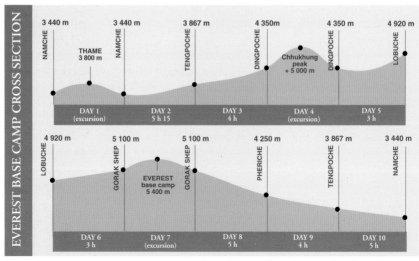

Traditional prayer flags juxtaposed with modern tents, a typical view of the Everest Base Camp.

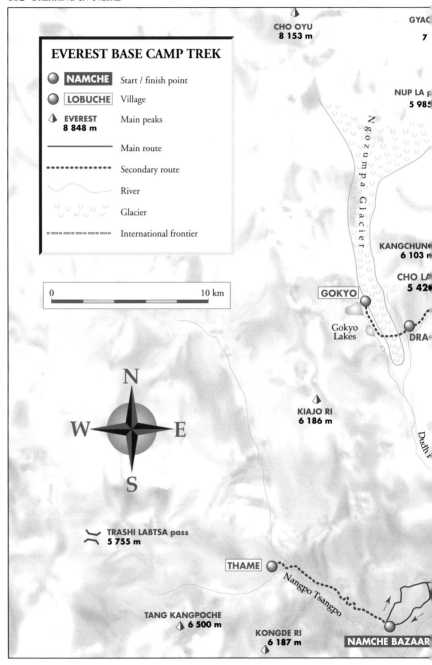

EVEREST BASE CAMP TREK

- 🔵 **NAMCHE**   Start / finish point
- 🔵 **LOBUCHE**   Village
- ⌂ **EVEREST 8 848 m**   Main peaks
- ───────   Main route
- ··············   Secondary route
- ∿∿∿   River
- ᵔ ᵔ ᵔ   Glacier
- ⊸⊶⊸⊶   International frontier

0   10 km

CHO OYU
8 153 m

GYAC
7

NUP LA p
5 985

Ngozumpa Glacier

KANGCHUN
6 103 n

CHO LA
5 420

GOKYO

Gokyo
Lakes

DRA

KIAJO RI
6 186 m

Dudh

N
W   E
S

TRASHI LABTSA pass
5 755 m

THAME

Nangpo Tsangpo

TANG KANGPOCHE
6 500 m

KONGDE RI
6 187 m

NAMCHE BAZAAR

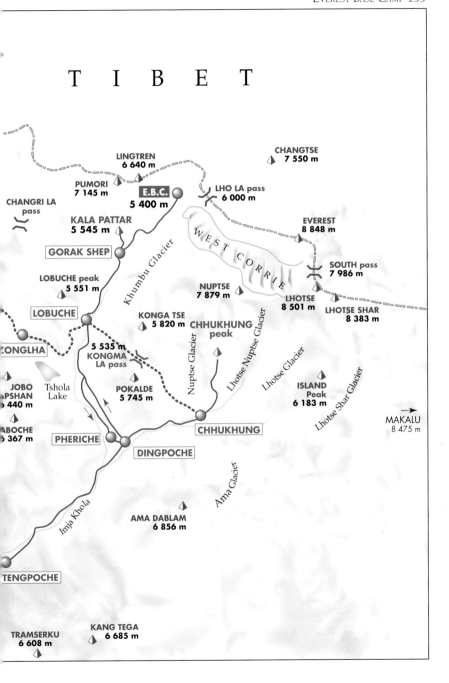

T I B E T

CHANGTSE
7 550 m

LINGTREN
6 640 m

PUMORI
7 145 m

LHO LA pass
6 000 m

E.B.C.
5 400 m

CHANGRI LA
pass

EVEREST
8 848 m

KALA PATTAR
5 545 m

WEST CORRIE

Khumbu Glacier

GORAK SHEP

SOUTH pass
7 986 m

LOBUCHE peak
5 551 m

NUPTSE
7 879 m

LHOTSE
8 501 m

LHOTSE SHAR
8 383 m

LOBUCHE

KONGA TSE
5 820 m

CHHUKHUNG
peak

Lhotse Nuptse Glacier

ONGLHA

5 535 m
KONGMA
LA pass

Nuptse Glacier

Lhotse Glacier

Lhotse Shar Glacier

JOBO
PSHAN
440 m

Tshola
Lake

POKALDE
5 745 m

ISLAND
Peak
6 183 m

MAKALU
8 475 m

ABOCHE
367 m

PHERICHE

CHHUKHUNG

Lhotse Shar Glacier

DINGPOCHE

Ama Glacier

Imja Khola

AMA DABLAM
6 856 m

TENGPOCHE

TRAMSERKU
6 608 m

KANG TEGA
6 685 m

This trek is hazardous during the winter, when snow blocks the route, and during the monsoon, when the peaks are covered with clouds throughout the day. The best time, therefore, is from March to May or though it is busier, from September to November.

This region, called the Solu Khumbu, includes some of the world's highest peaks, such as Everest (8,848 metres) also called Chomolungma by the Tibetans, or Sagarmatha by the Nepalese, Lhotse (8,501 metres), Lhotse Shar (8,383 metres), Makalu (8,475 metres) and Cho Oyu (8,153 metres).

This concentration of high mountains leads one to believe that the region is a desert of ice, but this is not so. This is the land of the Sherpas, a people originally from Tibet, who are traditionally farmers and cattle breeders. While they are better known the world over for their incredible physical strength and mountaineering skills, their customs and folklore are often overlooked. Those who visit this region will personally experience their hospitality, an aspect modern tourism has not changed.

Namche Bazaar is the starting point for this trek. You can either get there on foot from Jiri, as suggested in the previous itinerary, or by plane from Kathmandu to Lukla, a small town with a high altitude airport, one and a half days away from Namche Bazaar. (For this part of the route please read pages 128 and 129.)

We suggest that you book your ticket well in advance, since most people choose to fly and the aircraft can only accommodate 16 passengers. A return ticket costs US$166, payable in this currency. Ask for an open ticket and carefully check the date of reconfirmation. As this itinerary requires a minimum of fifteen days, don't book your return ticket before then.

Namche Bazaar

Those who visit Namche Bazar for the first time are enthralled by its beauty. Located in the midst of a mountainous cirque, 3,440 metres high, this is the capital of Khumbu and overlooks two large valleys - the Dudh Kosi and the Bhote Kosi (also called Nangpo Tsangpo). It is enclosed by several snowy peaks, with the Kongde Ri range towards the southwest, and Tramserku (6,608 metres) and Kang Tega (6,685 metres) towards the southeast.

Houses, arranged in a horseshoe pattern around the central chorten, make the village look even more picturesque. The surrounding slopes, too steep for cultivation, are dedicated to the gods. From the nearby gompa, songs and prayers sung by the lamas can be heard at regular hours.

Namche Bazaar is also the administrative centre of the district as well as the region's most important trading centre. It is also the tourist core of Khumbu. You will find a post-office (a letter to Europe takes about three weeks), a bank (which can even change travellers' cheques), a museum (featuring the traditional life and culture of the Sherpas and describing the National Park), and last but not least, a police station. There is also a military camp, as well as a small hydroelectric plant supplying electricity to most of the local lodges.

It is impossible to list all the lodges available, as new ones open almost every season. Among the nicest and most accessible is the Sherpa Trekker's Lodge, just above the chorten. The Buddha Lodge next door hosted Jimmy Carter during an official visit in 1985, and for a paltry sum you can sleep on the same bed the ex-President of the United States once used. A brass plaque and a few photographs commemorate the event.

There are plenty of shops too, where you can find anything from yak wool socks to Gore-Tex duffle coats; or from a dry goat carcass to instant noodles. Previous expedition teams sell their surplus equipment to shopkeepers who charge four times extra. Don't miss the weekly market, held every Saturday near the large rock at the entrance to the village.

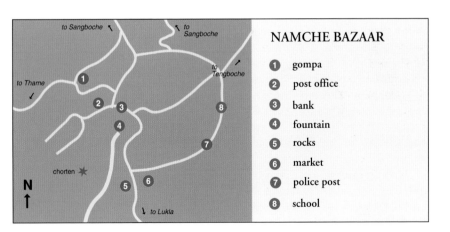

NAMCHE BAZAAR

1. gompa
2. post office
3. bank
4. fountain
5. rocks
6. market
7. police post
8. school

The First Day

FROM NAMCHE BAZAAR TO THAME (about 7 hours return)

At Namche Bazaar symptoms of altitude sickness could occur (see chapter on Health, page 28), especially if you took the direct flight to Lukla, and your body has not yet had the time to adjust to the height. Therefore, you should spend at least one day at the same altitude before you attempt to go higher. To make this obligatory halt more pleasant, we suggest the following excursion to the village of Thame, east of Namche Bazaar.

From Namche's gompa, the path on the left wends its way through large rocks engraved with the incantation Om mane padme hum, through a forest to enter the village of Phurte (3,480 metres). From here, go down to the bridge over the Kyajo Khola. The path follows the ridge of a hill, about 3,500 metres high, overlooking the Nangpo Tsangpo River. The forest disappears and the landscape is dominated by rocks and shrubs unlike the opposite side of the valley which is covered with pine trees. Cross the villages of Thamo (sometimes spelt Dramo) and Thomde. At the end of this village there is a crossroads, where it is easy to miss the right path. If in doubt, ask the way to the gompa of Thomde (run by nuns) which is on the way to Samde. The path going down to the river is part of an earlier itinerary still mentioned on maps, but now impenetrable because of heavy landslides.

After Samde, a steel suspension bridge crosses the Nangpo Tsangpo. On both sides of the cliff, there are two colourful paintings representing Guru Ringpoche and Green Tara, both important figures of the Buddhist pantheon. After the bridge, the slope which goes down to the torrent emerging from the Thengpo glacier is quite steep, so take care. Follow the stream up until you reach Thame (or Thame Og).

Located on a plateau 3,800 metres high, the village of Thame is distinguished by its unique architecture. Every house is two storeyed - the ground floor usually shelters animals while the upper floor has a large fireplace and is the common room for the family. In the frontyard, the Sherpas grow potatoes, their staple food. The two or three lodges you will find in Thame provide the sort of family atmosphere which Namche Bazar lacks.

Thirty minutes west of Thame is one of the region's most famous gompas. Each May, thousands of pilgrims flock to the monastery for the Mani Rimdu festival, the main celebration of the Buddhist calendar. But for most of the time, the place is quiet. To reach it, climb up to the chorten overlooking the village and follow the path bordered by a mani wall. Small houses that provide monks and hermits with shelter are scattered around the temple. For a small donation of a few rupees, you will be allowed to visit the prayer room. Ask to see the small printing workshop where some old collections of Sanskrit mantras are kept.

After the gompa, the path goes towards the Trashi Labtsa Pass (5,755 metres) which links the Khumbu Valley to the valley of Rolwaling. But that is another story.

The return trip from Namche Bazaar to Thame takes about six to seven hours. Make sure you take a raincoat, some water and food for the day. Alternatively, you can choose to stay overnight in Thame and have a chance to watch sunrise over Tang Kangpoche (6,500 metres), Kongde Ri (6,187 metres), and further away, Tramserku and Kang Tega.

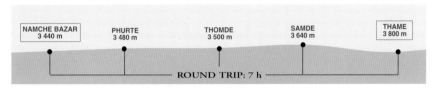

| NAMCHE BAZAR | PHURTE | THOMDE | SAMDE | THAME |
| 3 440 m | 3 480 m | 3 500 m | 3 640 m | 3 800 m |

ROUND TRIP: 7 h

The Second Day

FROM NAMCHE BAZAAR TO TENGPOCHE (about 5 hours and 15 minutes)
From the gompa, take the path on your right which climbs up alongside a barbed wired enclosure. Thirty minutes later, you will reach a small chorten. At this stage, the slope which was quite steep till now becomes gentler. Carry on climbing for another thirty minutes. Several small paths intersect the scrubland, all leading to the Syangboche altitude airstrip, 3,680 metres high. After a few bhattis, you will see the runway. This airport is mostly used by the cargo planes

and helicopters of the Asian Airlines Helicopter Company. A return ticket to Kathmandu costs about US$200.

The path enters a grove with a mani wall indicating a new junction. The path on the left leads to Khunde but you will have to take the path which is on your right. After fifteen minutes you will reach an imposing chorten sitting on top of a hill, 3,833 metres high. Going down to Khumjung (3,790 metres) which you will enter through a kani takes another thirty minutes. Walk beside the school built by the Edmund Hillary Foundation and keep to your right after the central chorten if you want to avoid the village. Khumjung's proximity to Namche Bazaar is perhaps why it has little to offer tourists except perhaps for a bakery producing delicious loaves of bread and cinnamon rolls.

The other attraction of the place is its gompa which is reputed to contain the scalp of the Yeti. True or false, nobody knows. No one can even prove it scientifically though everyone thinks - or pretends to think - that this piece of fur, hard as iron, belongs to the Abominable Snowman. For a small donation, the lama will show you the piece of the fur. And the young monks all have frightening stories to relate.

Shortly after Khumjung, there is another junction. The path which follows the ridge of the hill on the left leads to the Gokyo Lakes (see page 148), while the one on the right leads to the Tibetan hamlet of Sanasa (about 3,600 metres), thirty minutes away. For about ten minutes, the path overlooks the Dudh Kosi from an impressive height. Afterwards, you will walk through a pine forest until the village of Trashinga. The path continues to descend until Phunki (3,250 metres) where there are lodges on both sides of the suspension bridge.

After the bridge, the route leaves the Dudh Kosi Valley and goes along the valley of the Imja Khola. The slope is steep until the village of Tengpoche (sometimes spelt Thyangboche), built on top of a hill, 3,867 metres high, two and a half hours away. You will not find any water or bhattis on this route.

The entrance to Tengpoche is through an old kani and an imposing chorten. You then enter a large esplanade with, on your right, Khumbu's most famous gompa, built in the Twenties. This monastery has witnessed a series of disasters. It was destroyed once by an earthquake in 1933 and later by a fire in 1989. Since then, it has been rebuilt and restored by some of the country's best artists and looks startlingly new. You can also visit the Sherpa Cultural Centre, behind the monastery's main building, or attend one of the ceremonies performed by the monks of the Nyingmapa sect, also known as the 'Ancients'.

The Tashi Delek Lodge is probably the village's most comfortable hotel, with separate rooms as well as dormitory beds. It has hot water, excellent food and the view from the dining room is spectacular - you can see Ama Dablam, called 'mother's pendant' because of the big lump of snow which surmounts its main peak. Towards the northeast is Lhotse Shar (8,383 metres); towards the north, Everest; and towards the north-north-west, Taboche (6,367 metres).

If the Tashi Delek Lodge is fully booked, try the dormitory of the Trekker's Lodge, behind which lies a small cemetery where some Japanese mountaineers, who perished climbing Everest, are buried. At the end of the path leading to the Trekker's Lodge, you can see Cho Oyu (8,153 metres). Like Namche Bazaar, all the hotels in Tengpoche have electricity, which is provided by a small hydroelectric plant, which in turn receives water from a torrent flowing down Tramserku (6,608 metres), a large mountain overlooking the southern part of the village.

The Third Day

FROM TENGPOCHE TO DINGPOCHE (about 4 hours)

After going down through a rhododendron forest for fifteen minutes, you will find an imposing, contemporary structure, the Ama Dablam Lodge, from where there are magnificent views of Tengpoche. A few minutes later, you will reach the hamlet of Deboche (3,700 metres), just off the main track, which houses a monastery run by nuns. If you follow the path overlooking the Imja Khola for thirty minutes, you will reach a suspension bridge. Cross over and start climbing towards the village of Pangboche which is about an hour away.

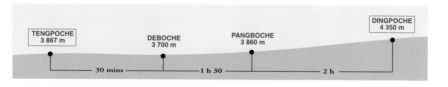

The vegetation from now on is dominated by stunted rhododendrons and thorny bushes, while the path follows a series of chortens and mani walls. The next kani you will go through marks the entrance to the village of Pangboche. The lower village (3,860 metres), where there are several lodges to have lunch in, is very near now. The upper village (3,985 metres) boasts of one of the oldest gompas of the region. The view of Ama Dablam is getting closer, while to the south you can still see Tramserku and Kang Tega.

After Pangboche, the path follows the west bank of the Imja Khola for thirty minutes, at an average altitude of 4,000 metres. A steep, narrow path leads to the hamlet of Somare with its three or four basic lodges. Then the slope becomes gentle till Orsho, where you will find the last lodge before Dingpoche. The path ascends steadily until it reaches a large rock perched at a junction. The altitude here is 4,100 metres. Arrows painted in red on the rock point towards the direction of Pheriche village on the left, and Dingpoche.

Another hour's climb will take you to Dingpoche whose entrance is marked by three chortens, one above the other. The average altitude of the village is 4,350 metres. There are several lodges but most of them only have dormitory beds to offer, except for the Sonam Friendship Lodge and Restaurant which has two tiny individual bedrooms and about twenty dormitory beds. Now you are almost at the base of Ama Dablam.

The Fourth Day

AROUND DINGPOCHE
Having reached the height of 4,300 metres it is wise to take a break and ensure that your body adapts to the altitude. This also provides an opportunity to explore the valley of the Imja Khola where more than one excursion is possible.

The most interesting is probably the one to Chhukhung Peak, more than 5,000 metres high. A guide is essential as this is also the most difficult excursion as the path is hard to follow and can be dangerous at times. For the more cautious trekker, there is the excursion to Imja Tse Base Camp, also called Mount Island (6,183 metres), which seals the extreme east-end of the valley. Others can

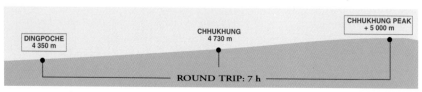

CHHUKHUNG PEAK
+ 5 000 m

CHHUKHUNG
4 730 m

DINGPOCHE
4 350 m

ROUND TRIP: 7 h

A winter view of Namche Bazar, capital of Khumbu.

choose to go to the Lhotse Shar Base Camp at the bottom of its southern slope. These two walks are through the moraines left by the glaciers flowing down the mountains.

All these excursions start the same way, through the hamlet of Chhukhung (4,730 metres), the last inhabited village of the valley, about two hours away from Dingpoche. The path easily follows the Imja Khola through a terrain of rocks and pastures. You will find several lodges in Chhukhung where you can have breakfast before you start climbing Chhukhung Peak.

The path proceeds in the northern direction between the Nuptse and Lhotse Nuptse glaciers. The track is difficult to follow as it is mostly covered with snow. Whatever the season, snowfalls are frequent at this altitude.

Chhukhung Peak is not mentioned on any map, so it is difficult to evaluate its exact altitude. However, the ascension unveils a grand view of the surrounding mountains - Ama Dablam towards the south; Mount Island towards the east; Lhotse Shar, Lhotse and Nuptse (7,879 metres) to the north. Further away, you can see Pokalde (5,745 metres); Konga Tse (5,820 metres); and between the two, the Kongma La (5,535 metres) which links the valleys of Chhukhung and Lobuche. Crossing this pass demands mountaineering rather than trekking skills.

The Fifth Day

From Dingpoche to Lobuche (about 3 hours)

Climb to the chorten overlooking Dingpoche, at an altitude of about 4,410 metres. You will then reach a huge plateau with pastures from where you can see Pheriche village down in the valley. Crossing this plateau will take about an hour. The descent is easy with a magnificent view just before you. Behind you, looms Ama Dablam and an endless series of 6,000-metre-high peaks including Tramserku and Kang Tega. On your left, the icy slopes of Taboche (6,367 metres) and Jobo Lhapshan (6,440 metres) gleam in the sun, while on your right, the massif Pokalde and Lobuche Peak (5,551 metres) are visible.

The path goes down to a small wooden bridge which leads to the few bhattis of Duglha (4,620 metres). Stop here for lunch as it is the last stopover until Lobuche.

The path leads up to a sort of pass scattered with cairns and engraved rocks. According to the maps, the place you will reach after an hour of climbing is the ultimate boundary of the Khumbu glacier which comes down from Everest.

You will then have to follow the ridge of a moraine. Although the difference in altitude is not great, progress along this part of the route is quite slow because of the high altitude. It will therefore take you another hour to reach Lobuche. The latter is less of a village and more of a group of five or six lodges offering basic facilities. None of them have separate rooms, only large dormitories, so the earlier you get there the better is your chance to choose a bed.

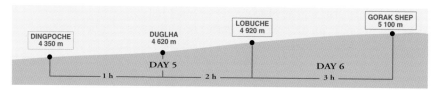

The Sixth Day

FROM LOBUCHE TO GORAK SHEP (about 3 hours)

Some trekkers prefer to bypass Lobuche and go directly to Gorak Shep, the last habitation before the Everest Base Camp. This place, at the base of Kala Pattar at about 5,100 metres, is in fact only three hours from Lobuche. However, to make sure that your body gets acclimatised to the altitude, we suggest that you stop in Lobuche.

The first half of the route is rather easy but it soon becomes rocky, thereby forcing you to undertake a series of ascents and descents.

If covered with snow, the path may also be difficult to follow, so it is better to either take a local guide or join another group. There are three lodges in Gorak Shep, all of which offer basic accommodation and food. But what more can you expect at this altitude?

The Seventh Day

KALA PATTAR AND EVEREST BASE CAMP

To give you an idea of what awaits you, observe the path which leads to Kala Pattar (or 'black rock') from the window of any of the lodges. It will take you three hours to climb before you reach the top marked with cairns and a sign indicating the altitude - 5,545 metres. Make sure you leave at an appropriate time. If you reach too early, it is likely that you may freeze while waiting for the sun to rise.

There are no words to describe the magical vistas that will unfold before you. To give you some idea, here are some of the peaks that you can see - Tramserku,

Kang Tega and Ama Dablam to the south; Makalu Peak further away towards the east; closer are Nuptse, Lhotse and the black pyramid of Mount Everest. Further away, you can also see Changtse (7,550 metres) in Tibet. Within the borders of Nepal, stands Lingtren (6,640 metres) beside Pumori, overlooking Kala Pattar. Then comes the Chang Ri range, sealing the horizon to the west, and last but not least, Jobo Lhapshan and Taboche.

Return to Gorak Shep for lunch, it is time now to prepare for Everest Base Camp which is about three hours away, at an elevation of 5,400 metres. Follow the small glacial lake below the lodges until you reach a stele commemorating those mountaineers who died climbing Everest. After a steep slope, the path enters the moraine of the Khumbu glacier. It is easy to get lost among the large rocks so it is best to follow the cairns. You will soon reach a glacial area with strange concretions. Just in front of you, you can see a wall of seracs leading to Lho La (6,000 metres) in Tibet. Depending on the season, you may meet a couple of other expeditions along the way.

If you follow the colourful little flags placed by previous trekkers you will soon find yourself at the bottom of the icefall coming down from the west coomb. Though Everest is very close, you will not be able to see it. Don't forget that you are now in the mountaineers' kingdom. Or as the Nepalese believe, in the kingdom of the Gods.

Everest, in the background, as seen from Kala Pattar

Everest

Is Everest really the highest mountain in the world? This has been a much debated subject as some people claim that Chogori (or K2), in the Karakorum range in Pakistan, is actually higher. However, on 20 April 1993, a Franco-Italian expedition lead by the French mountaineer, Benoît Chamoux, conducted the first satellite measurement of Everest and confirmed that at 8,846 metres it is actually ten centimetres higher than K2. His measurement, however, showed that Everest is two metres shorter than commonly thought.

Since the beginning of time, both Tibetans and Sherpas have called Everest, Chomolungma, or 'the Mother Goddess'. The name Everest only came into existence in 1856, when the British, less romantic than the mountain people, wanted to mark their respect for Sir George Everest, the ex-Surveyor-General of India, and so called the mountain after him. To counter British cultural imperialism, the Nepalese came up with a third name, Sagarmatha, which is only used locally.

Whatever the name, this mountain never leaves anyone indifferent. Since its conquest in 1953, more than 600 mountaineers from all over the world have scaled its summit, most of them from its Nepalese side. Despite the fact that the Nepalese government has installed expensive rights of passage, there is a long waiting list and candidates have to wait several years before they can get the authorisation to climb. In May 1994 for instance, no less than four expeditions (one from Japan, one from New Zealand and two from the United States) were 'queuing' up at the base camp. The impact on the environment is also evident. According to the Sagarmatha Pollution Control Project, the organisation responsible for cleaning the area, 12,824 kilos of rubbish were collected from the base camp in 1993. Since then, Everest is commonly dubbed as the 'highest rubbish bin of the world'.

Sherpas at the Everest Base Camp

Days 8, 9 and 10 Back to Namche Bazaar

The return trip from Gorak Shep to Namche Bazaar is the same as the route from Namche to Gorak Shep as there is no other alternative. However, the trip takes only three days instead of five.

On the first day, stop for lunch at Lobuche. After Duglha, instead of going up to the plateau towards Dingpoche, walk directly to the base of the valley in the direction of Pheriche (4,250 metres) where you can stay overnight. The difference of altitude is about 850 metres. The second stage is from Pheriche to Tengpoche. The latter is about 400 metres lower in altitude and takes about four to five hours to cover the distance. The last stage of the route is a slight climb between Deboche and Tengpoche. On the third day, there is a long descent down to the hamlet of Sanasa, from where you can either return to Namche via Khumjung, or take the path following the east side of the hill. This route is different from the earlier one and provides a beautiful perspective of the Dudh Kosi Valley.

From Namche, you can reach Lukla on the same day although it means walking continuously for six hours. You may prefer to stop at Phakding again (see pages 128 and 129).

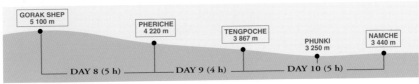

Tengpoche monastery with Ama Dablam in the horizon.

From Lobuche to Gokyo through the Cho La Pass

For trekkers who wish to go directly from the Everest Base Camp to the base camp leading to the Gokyo Lakes, described in the next chapter, there is a short cut linking Lobuche to Gokyo. This alternative itinerary goes through the Cho La pass, 5,420 metres high.

While this is a rather difficult route, new lodges set up along the trail in tourist season make it possible for the fit and the well equipped to complete in one long day. Bring warm clothing and some extra food, and do not attempt the pass if the weather looks threatening.

When you leave Lobuche, follow the west side of the valley up to 5,200 metres. You can see Duglha and the Tshola lakes down in the valley. Enter the valley that leads to Dzonglha where you will see some old huts scattered along a narrow plateau lying at the bottom of Jobo Lhapshan.

Start early next morning as a long walk awaits you. Follow the cairns leading to the very heart of the valley until the path suddenly goes up the hill. It soon reaches the first ledge right at the end of the glacier. Keep to the south side of the ridge to avoid crevasses. If the weather is fine, this part of the route should not take you more than an hour.

The descent of the west side, on a scree covered slope, is quite steep. After crossing the first moraine climb up to the point shown at 5,189 on the Schneider map. This is the start of a long climb down along a torrent until you reach the hamlet of Dragnag (4,690 metres) where you can find a lodge.

You have to pass the final stretch of the moraine of the Ngozumpa glacier, the largest in Nepal, before you ultimately reach the second Gokyo Lake. The village is only an hour away now, to the north.

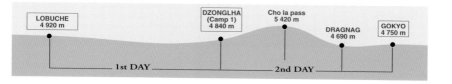

Gokyo Lakes

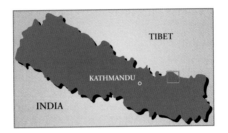

Introduction

Three large valleys cut across the Solu Khumbu region from the north to the south - the Nangpo Tsangpo Valley leads to Tibet and is forbidden to trekkers; the Lobuche Valley, described in the previous chapter, leads to Everest Base Camp; and the Dudh Kosi Valley whose source is in Nepal's most important glacier, the Ngozumpa. If one goes up the Dudh Kosi River, the 'milky river', one comes to the sacred lakes of Gokyo.

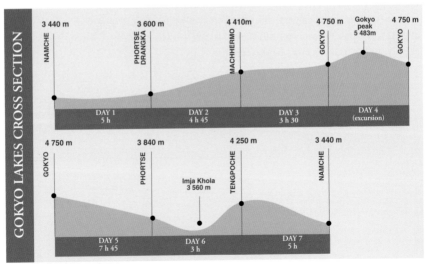

Slightly less popular than the more prestigious trek to Everest, this itinerary offers equally stunning views, but is less crowded.

The final destination of the trek is the village of Gokyo (4,750 metres), by the banks of the third and also the largest lake. These lakes, called tsho in the Sherpa dialect, have a deep religious significance for both Buddhists and Hindus, although they attract fewer pilgrims than Gosain Kund (see page 98).

The village is overlooked by the Gokyo Ri or Gokyo Peak, a kind of grassy hill inhabited only by yaks and danphes or the Impeyan pheasant. The view from its summit is more or less similar to that of Kala Pattar.

Furthermore, the trek to the sacred Gokyo Lakes is shorter and does not go as high as the Everest Base Camp. Yet, this trek is moderately difficult and requires some trekking experience.

The following pages describe seven days of a 'loop' itinerary from Namche Bazaar. To recap - to reach Namche from Kathmandu, you can either walk, via Jiri, following the itinerary on page 120, or you can fly to Lukla, as described on page 134. If you fly, add an extra day and a half to walk to Namche, plus another day to adjust to the altitude (see page 135). On the whole, you will need at least twelve days to cover the full itinerary.

An alternative itinerary, or short cut between the valleys of Gokyo and Lobuche, is also described on page 147 for those who wish to combine the Everest Base Camp and the sacred Gokyo Lakes treks.

Gyachung Kang and Ngozumpa glacier as seen from Gokyo Peak.

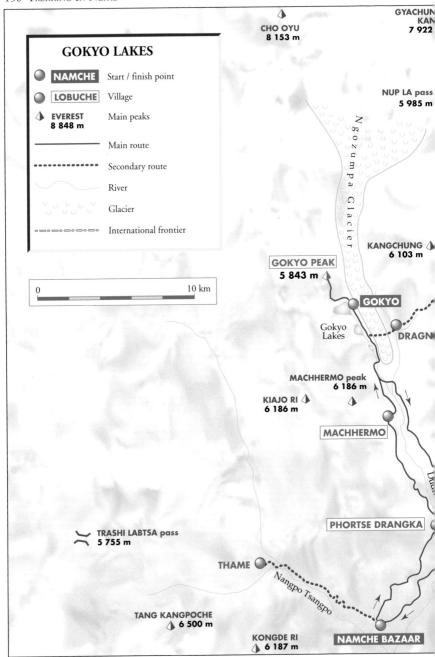

GOKYO LAKES

- **NAMCHE** — Start / finish point
- **LOBUCHE** — Village
- **EVEREST 8 848 m** — Main peaks
- Main route
- Secondary route
- River
- Glacier
- International frontier

0   10 km

CHO OYU
8 153 m

GYACHUN KAN
7 922

NUP LA pass
5 985 m

Ngozumpa Glacier

KANGCHUNG
6 103 m

GOKYO PEAK
5 843 m

GOKYO

Gokyo
Lakes

DRAGN

MACHHERMO peak
6 186 m

KIAJO RI
6 186 m

MACHHERMO

TRASHI LABTSA pass
5 755 m

PHORTSE DRANGKA

THAME

Nangpo Tsangpo

TANG KANGPOCHE
6 500 m

KONGDE RI
6 187 m

NAMCHE BAZAAR

T I B E T

CHANGTSE
7 550 m

LINGTREN
6 640 m

PUMORI
7 145 m

LHO LA pass
6 000 m

NGRI LA
pass

KALA PATTAR
5 545 m

EVEREST
8 848 m

WEST CORRIE

Khumbu Glacier

LA pass
420 m

LOBUCHE peak
5 551 m

SOUTH pass
7 986 m

NUPTSE
7 879 m

LHOTSE
8 501 m

LHOTSE SHAR
8 383 m

LOBUCHE

KONGA TSE
5 820 m

NGLHA

KONGMA
LA pass
5 535 m

Nuptse Glacier

Lhotse Nuptse Glacier

Lhotse Glacier

OBO
HAN
40 m

Tshola
Lake

POKALDE
5 745 m

ISLAND
Peak
6 183 m

Lhotse Shar Glacier

MAKALU
8 475 m

OCHE
67 m

Ama Glacier

RTSE

Imja Khola

AMA DABLAM
6 856 m

N

TENGPOCHE

W

E

S

RAMSERKU
6 608 m

KANG TEGA
6 685 m

The First Day

From Namche Bazaar to Phortse Drangka (about 5 hours)
Leave Namche along the direction of the gompa and turn right after the large
rocks engraved with Buddhist images. It takes about an hour's steep climb to
reach the Khumbila Guest House, one of the few habitations around Syangboche
airstrip, at 3,680 metres.

Turn left towards Khunde (3,840 metres) after the landing runway. There is a
yak farm followed by a forest plateau, at a height of 3,865 metres. From here,
going down to the village will take you forty five minutes. The hospital at
Khunde, the only one in the whole region, owes its existence to the Edmund
Hillary Foundation. A consultation costs US$10 for tourists, and Rs10 for
Nepalese patients.

Go in the direction of Khumjung (3,790 metres), about fifteen minutes away.
The village's gompa contains, among other things, the scalp of the yeti (see page
138). Soon after Khumjung, you will reach a junction. The path going down
leads to the Tibetan hamlet of Sanasa, and then on to Everest. To go to Gokyo
there is a path on the left with a flight of steps moving up the cliff. The path is
precipitous but not really dangerous. However, it will take you at least two hours
to climb and reach an altitude of 3,973 metres as indicated by a large chorten,
from where you have beautiful views of the Tengpoche monastery and the green
Phortse plateau. There are two or three lodges, including the Top Hill and the
Snow View, where you can have lunch.

You only have an hour of steep descent to reach Phortse Drangka (3,600
metres) - or Porche Tanka as mentioned on some signs outside the two lodges
overlooking the river. These shelters only have dormitory-type accommodation
and are quite dirty. You may prefer to carry on until the next stop, Dole, where
the accommodation is more acceptable. The other advantage is that it will
shorten the next day's walk.

If you feel like a rest, Phortse Drangka offers superb views of Tramserku
(6,608 metres), Kang Tega (6,685 metres) and Taboche (6,367 metres).

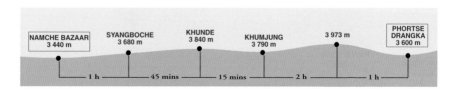

The Second Day

FROM PHORTSE DRANGKA TO MACHHERMO (about 4 hours and 45 minutes)
The path goes through the middle of a forest and offers the first view of Cho Oyu
Peak (8,153 metres). Thirty minutes later you will reach the police station where
you must have your trekking permit checked. Dole (4,040 metres), an hour and
a half away, has very pleasant lodges where you can have lunch.

Dole also marks the end of the forest. Thereafter you will walk across a rocky
terrain scattered with a few dwarf rhododendrons. At the end of the village, you
will have to cross a narrow stream which means that you must first go down and
then climb up to the other side. For two hours the path follows the 4,320-metre-
altitude line until it reaches Luza. The village of Machhermo (4,410 metres) is
only forty five minutes away. Two basic but comfortable lodges offer only dormitory beds. Climbing Machhermo Peak (5,328 metres), which overlooks the
village, is of little interest.

The Third Day

FROM MACHHERMO TO GOKYO (about 3 hours and 30 minutes)
After a short, thirty-minute climb you will reach a high plateau with the hamlet
of Pangka (4,480 metres). Follow the western bank of the Dudh Kosi. On the
opposite side you can see the village of Na.

Follow the stream up, cross a small bridge so that you can walk across a large
rocky outcrop. The path is marked with cairns. Leave the banks of the Dudh
Kosi which by now has turned milky in colour, hence its name, and follow one
of its tributaries which leads to a small lake. The path continues to go down until
it reaches a second, larger lake. By following its bank you will come to some iron
bars announcing Gokyo Lake.

The most comfortable lodges are the Gokyo Resort Lodge and the Gokyo Guest
House, an imposing edifice with a view over the lake, with dormitories for eight
people. You will have the choice between local Nepalese and international food.

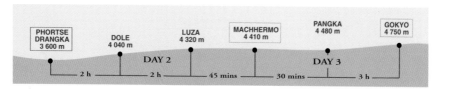

The Fourth Day

AROUND GOKYO

The excursion to the Gokyo Peak usually starts early in the morning. Take water and food. The path starts from the northern bank of the lake, and goes through a network of branches. The climb is quite steep for thirty minutes. It is followed by an hour-long walk across a grassy slope where yaks graze. The path is shown by cairns which rise up from between the rocks. By this time the climb becomes

tough once again and it will take you an hour to reach the top with its traditional prayer flags. To have the best view, follow the ridge up to the 5,483-metre altitude point - towards the north, an imposing range of mountains marks the border with Tibet. Some of the highest peaks, from the west to east, are - Cho Oyu (8,153 metres), Gyachung Kang (7,922 metres), then the dome of Everest (8,848 metres), Lhotse (8,501 metres) and further away, Makalu (8,475 metres).

Below, you can see the entire Ngozumpa glacial system, right down to its final moraine. During the two hour descent, you can enjoy, right in front of you, a superb view of Gokyo Lake, turquoise in colour or, depending upon the season, frozen.

In the afternoon, you can walk around the lake and examine the different cairns scattered along its banks. Remember to circumambulate from the left to the right as is the Buddhist custom, based on the direction the earth moves aound the sun.

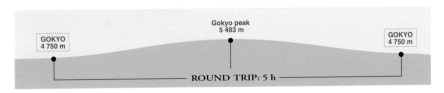

GOKYO
4 750 m

Gokyo peak
5 483 m

GOKYO
4 750 m

ROUND TRIP: 5 h

(Above)...and during the monsoon.
(Left) Gokyo Lake in spring...

The Fifth Day

From Gokyo to Phortse (around 7 hours 45 minutes)

To return, go back the same way you had come for the first two hours, until you reach a junction. This time, instead of going up to Pangka, go down towards the banks of the Dudh Kosi. Cross the river over a wooden bridge and walk up to the village of Na (4,480 metres). You will now have to cross a new river, the Na Khola. Walk until you reach the eastern bank of the Dudh Kosi, forty five minutes away. The path goes up slowly for about two hours until it reaches the hamlet of Thare (4,360 metres) where you can have lunch.

After Thare, the path goes up and down at an average altitude of 4,400 metres. It takes two hours to reach the village of Konar (4,250 metres), and another hour to reach the high Phortse plateau (3,840 metres). Since Phortse is not very popular among tourists, it only has two lodges - the Solu Khumbu Lodge, set in the upper village, and Namaste Lodge, with its name painted in large, bold letters on the roof. This will be a rather long though somewhat easy day, as the path goes downhill most of the time.

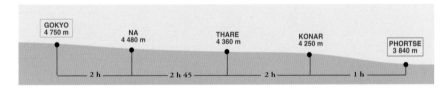

GOKYO 4 750 m — NA 4 480 m — THARE 4 360 m — KONAR 4 250 m — PHORTSE 3 840 m

2 h — 2 h 45 — 2 h — 1 h

Gokyo Peak, and on the right, Cho Oyu.

The Sixth Day

FROM PHORTSE TO TENGPOCHE (around 3 hours)
Unlike the previous day, this will be shorter but quite difficult considering the configuration of the route. It starts with the crossing of the Phortse plateau from the west to the east. Then the path goes straight down a steep slope, towards the banks of the
. The difference of altitude is 300 metres and it should not take you more than an hour and a half.

Unfortunately, to reach the village of Tengpoche, at 3,867 metres, you will have to re-climb the 300 metres. This part of the route goes through what was once a magnificent forest, but is now denuded because most of the trees have been cut to supply the local demand for fuel.

A steep and difficult one hour climb, which can be further aggravated by rain or snow, will take you to Tengpoche. From here you can join the itinerary to the Everest Base Camp. See page 138 for details about Tengpoche and its famous gompa.

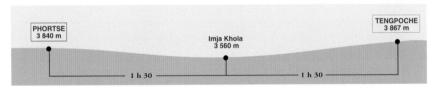

The Seventh Day

FROM TENGPOCHE TO NAMCHE BAZAAR (around 5 hours)
The route from Tengpoche to Namche Bazaar is described in detail on the second day of the previous itinerary. It will take you slightly less time than indicated as the route goes downhill most of the time.

From Jumla To Lake Rara

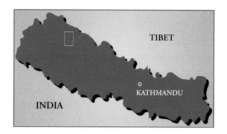

Introduction

Going to Lake Rara is like going to Nepal's 'far west' because not only does the region lie to the extreme west of Kathmandu, 360 kilometres away, but also because its wild areas (snowy mountains, peaks covered with pine trees, impetuous torrents) brings to mind the North American Far West. Hence, the region is often dubbed as 'Nepal's Rocky Mountains'.

The comparison stops here. Rather than cowboys, the region is mostly inhabited by isolated rural communities. The people who live in this region are neither Gurung nor Sherpa, whose features and customs are of Tibetan descent. They are instead a mix of Brahmans, Chhetris and Thakuris, mostly of Indian origin, as their features, lifestyle and religion suggest. Interestingly, almost every village is completely autonomous with different peoples and traditions. The Thakuris or 'royal caste' for instance, have given Nepal its current ruling dynasty.

Jumla, the main town of the region and in fact its only one, is also the starting point of the trek. There are only a few lodges that offer basic facilities. The region's distance from Kathmandu coupled with the absence of prestigious peaks to climb, perhaps explains why there is no tourist infrastructure. There are hardly any lodges and restaurants outside Jumla. Local guides and porters are also difficult to find. Besides, very few people can speak English.

For all these reasons, the trek to Lake Rara is off the beaten track. The simplest solution - but also the most expensive - is to ask a travel agency in Kathmandu to organise the whole trip for you. It will cost you a minimum of US$40 per day, per person.

Lake Rara as seen from Murma Peak.

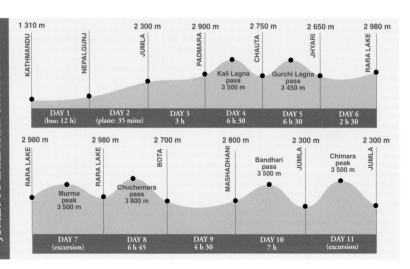

1 310 m	2 300 m	2 900 m	2 750 m	2 650 m	2 980 m
KATHMANDU	NEPALGUNJ	JUMLA	PADMARA	CHAUTA	JHYARI	RARA LAKE

Kali Lagna pass 3 500 m

Gurchi Lagna pass 3 450 m

| DAY 1 (bus: 12 h) | DAY 2 (plane: 35 mins) | DAY 3 3 h | DAY 4 6 h 30 | DAY 5 6 h 30 | DAY 6 2 h 30 |

2 980 m	2 980 m	2 700 m	2 800 m	2 300 m	2 300 m
RARA LAKE	RARA LAKE	BOTA	MASHADHANI	JUMLA	JUMLA

Murma peak 3 500 m

Chuchemara pass 3 800 m

Bandhari pass 3 500 m

Chimara peak 3 500 m

| DAY 7 (excursion) | DAY 8 6 h 45 | DAY 9 4 h 30 | DAY 10 7 h | DAY 11 (excursion) |

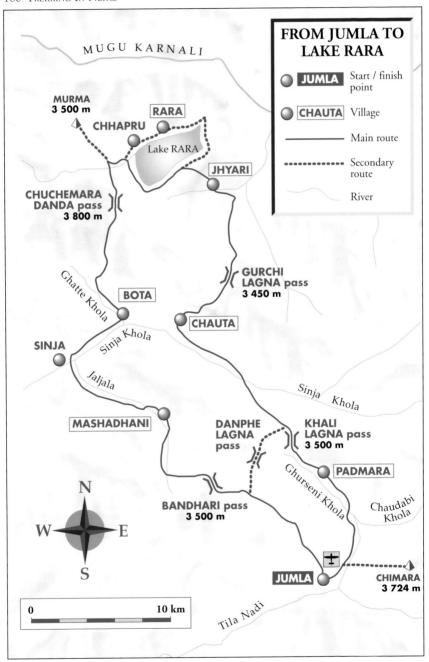

MUGU KARNALI

FROM JUMLA TO LAKE RARA

JUMLA Start / finish point

CHAUTA Village

Main route

Secondary route

River

MURMA 3 500 m

CHHAPRU

RARA

Lake RARA

JHYARI

CHUCHEMARA DANDA pass 3 800 m

GURCHI LAGNA pass 3 450 m

Ghatte Khola

BOTA

CHAUTA

SINJA

Sinja Khola

Jaljala

Sinja Khola

MASHADHANI

DANPHE LAGNA pass

KHALI LAGNA pass 3 500 m

PADMARA

Ghurseni Khola

Chaudabi Khola

BANDHARI pass 3 500 m

N

W E

S

JUMLA

CHIMARA 3 724 m

0   10 km

Tila Nadi

The approach to the village of Padmara.

You could also organise it yourself, but this will mean finding your own guide, renting the equipment (such as a tent, portable gas cooker, etc) and carrying enough food. For more information read the sections How To Choose A Trek, starting on page 20.

The following itinerary requires fifteen days, including the return.

The First Day

FROM KATHMANDU TO NEPALGUNJ (bus: about 12 hours)

Somehow, Jumla seems like the end of the world and although it is the entrance to Lake Rara, there is no direct road from Kathmandu. There are several daily flights though operated by Royal Nepal Airlines Corporation (RNAC). A one way ticket costs US$122, payable in US dollars. As it happens, RNAC gives discounts as well, but you will have to enquire at the domestic flights office in Kathmandu (see map of Kathmandu, page 18–19). A practical compromise - although it is time-consuming and tiring - would be to take a bus from Kathmandu to Nepalgunj, in the Terai region in southern Nepal, and from here fly to Jumla.

Book your seat on the bus the day before departure from the Gongabu bus terminal, north of Kathmandu, about twenty minutes from Thamel. The seats that provide the most space are 1 and 2 A, near the door. Buses depart daily at 5 pm and 7 pm. The drive to Nepalgunj, 460 kilometres away, takes twelve hours or all night. Until Mugling, the road is the same as the one going to Pokhara (see Around the Annapurnas, page 38). The bus then leaves the Prithvi Highway to take the Mahendra Highway going south, stopping at Narayangadh for dinner. Thereafter, the road leaves the mountainous terrain and crosses the Terai plains from the east to the west. Although it is a straight road, it is difficult to sleep as the bus makes frequent stops throughout the journey to let passengers get in and out. Sometimes, even in the middle of the night, the driver rouses a monk or priest to ask him to pray for the safety of the bus and its passengers. What is more, the radio blares throughout and it is very likely that you will be exhausted by the time you reach Nepalgunj.

Nepalgunj is a big market town sprawled along the main road, hardly eight kilometres from the Indian border. It is not only very hot, but also very dusty and infested with mosquitoes. Hotels are very basic. Before you check in, make sure the room has at least a shower (check the water), an electric fan and a mosquito net over the bed.

Because of the uncertainity of road transportation in Nepal, it is better to book your flight for the day after you arrive in Nepalgunj. You might miss your flight if your schedule is tighter. Daily flights connect Nepalgunj to Jumla. A one way ticket costs US$44. You can buy it from the RNAC office on the main road (ask a rickshaw to take you), but we suggest that you make the reservation at Kathmandu. Ask for an open return ticket so that you can reconfirm at Jumla.

For those who don't mind the inconvenience it is also possible to go from Nepalgunj to Surkhet by bus and then to walk for five days to reach Jumla.

The Second Day

FROM NEPALGUNJ TO JUMLA (by plane: about 35 minutes)
Take a rickshaw or a horse carriage to the airport, as it is some distance from the city centre. The fare should be about Rs50 and should not take you more than thirty minutes. There are a few basic lodges around the airport, also a bar within the airport complex where you can have breakfast.

Theoretically the first flight to Jumla is at 6.30 am but delays are frequent. Check in is an hour before departure. Airport tax is Rs20. The flight only lasts thirty five minutes which makes the contrast between the two locations even more striking.

Located in the Tila Nadi Valley, at a height of 2,300 metres, Jumla is the main town of the district of the same name. With its paved main road, double terraced houses, green landscape, the town retains its rural flavour. In addition to being an important market place for the whole region, it also houses the region's administrative offices, a hospital, a bank, a post-office, a police station, an army post, and even a prison in a dilapidated building about to collapse.

The town also has a small community of foreigners working on a conservation project of the Karnali Basin. This small settlement, or 'foreign country', as the locals call it, is about fifteen minutes away from the northern part of the village. As mentioned earlier, Jumla only has four or five lodges. We recommend the Snow View Hotel where both the atmosphere and food are good.

The Third Day

FROM JUMLA TO PADMARA (about 3 hours)
Before you leave make sure that you have enough small change as you will not be able to change a 100-rupee banknote elsewhere. The bank opens at 10.30 am. Do a little shopping as well (instant soups, biscuits, chocolate) as you will not find many shops later.

To leave Jumla, go back to the airport and follow the Chaudabise Khola. The path goes slowly up along a hill that joins the Ghurseni Khola, one of the tributaries of the Chaudabise Khola, in a northwest direction.

After forty five minutes, you will see a large building with a sloping roof - very rare for the region. This is the Rajukot experimental farm, and you will notice superb apple trees nearby. The harvesting of the fruits takes place in October/November.

Narayan Hotel, the first lodge in the village of Urtu Chauta (2,500 metres), provides the typical menu - dal bhat for all meals.

Urtu Chauta controls two valleys - the one on the right leads to Dolpo. Take the one on the left and walk along the Khriya Khola until you reach a small bridge facing a huge natural cave. You will soon reach a watermill at the point where the path branches off in two directions. The path on the right leads to the hamlets of Rini and Ghorsina. But you should take the one on the left which will lead you without any difficulty directly to Padmara, about two hours away.

Padmara (2,900 metres) has no lodge or restaurant but you can ask - with the help of your guide - the local people to let you camp for the night as well as provide a hot meal. If you are alone you will have to use body language which will create a sensation among the villagers who are unused to foreigners. Do not panic if a crowd surrounds and scrutinizes you and your belongings. Just keep quiet and smile and their curiosity will soon disappear. Ask for permission before you take any photographs. All this is part of the culture shock that makes such travel interesting.

JUMLA 2 300 m — URTU CHAUTA 2 500 m — PADMARA 2 900 m — 1 h — 2 h

The Fourth Day

FROM PADMARA TO CHAUTA (about 6 hours and 30 minutes)
Take the western direction and climb a gentle slope for about an hour through
wheat fields and sheepfolds. You may encounter a herd of goats laden with bags
of salt, a mode of transportation seen only in western parts of Nepal and Tibet.

Later, the slope becomes more arduous and it takes at least forty five minutes
to reach the first pass, the Khali Lagna at 3,500 metres. In winter, it may be
covered with snow. At the top of the pass, there is another small path on your
left, which leads to the Danphe Lagna pass, part of another possible itinerary
from Jumla. The main path carries on among fields until Tharmare, about twenty
minutes away.

In Tharmare you will only find two indifferent shelters where local shepherds
sometimes stop. The food also is basic - chapatis or rotis, potatoes and black tea.
The path suddenly goes down through the middle of a forest of pine and birch. It
takes about an hour to reach a vast grassland which faces very high cliffs on the
opposite side of the Sinja Khola. Go down for another twenty minutes until you
reach the river. Cross over and fifteen minutes later you will reach the hamlet of
Nyurigadh where there are two bhattis.

The path follows the east bank of the river, the flow of which will force you to
undertake several ascents and descents. The river ends in a very narrow gorge
which entails a forty five minute climb up a very steep slope before you can go
down again towards a small valley irrigated by the Kabra Khola. An even steeper
slope will lead you to a village of the same name, about twenty minutes away.

From Kabra, the path goes up for thirty minutes until the hamlet of Bhada
(Naulekh for the Tibetans) after which it flattens again and goes through fields
for forty minutes before descending to the village of Chauta, twenty minutes
away. Clustered at the bottom of the Chauta Khola Valley, which later on meets
the Sinja Khola, Chauta has two restaurants and a few rooms on rent. Try the
local speciality, a kind of red rice called rato bhat.

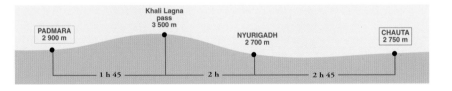

The Fifth Day

FROM CHAUTA TO JHYARI (about 6 hours 30 minutes)

Go towards the north along the Chauta Khola for about an hour to reach the hamlet of Bhulbhule where you will find two lodges offering only dal bhat and black tea. At the end of the village, a police station marks the entrance to the Rara National Park. Show your trekking permit as well as your entry ticket to the park.

For the next thirty minutes, the path is flat until it reaches a grassland framed by high rocks. Cross this mountainous cirque and follow the main track which leads to the Gurchi Lagna Pass (3,450 metres). The slope is not too steep and it only takes forty five minutes to reach the top for a superb view of the Himalayan range along the border with Tibet.

The steep descent from the pass to the next crossroads takes about forty five minutes. A signpost written in English and Nepali, indicates the route to Rara via Jhyari. The main path goes towards the village of Pina at the base of the valley, while a minor pathway through a superb pine forest goes up and down along the ridge of a hill.

There is another twenty minute climb starting from the next junction - not very well indicated. You must take the narrow path on the left which goes amidst fields and leads to a small clearing used as a helipad.

Go down to the Shyaljara River, cross over before starting the last ascent of the day, which will lead you to Jhyari village. Like Padmara, Jhyari (2,650 metres) does not provide any accommodation and you will have to negotiate once again with the local peasants to set up your camp for the night. With the help of your guide you may also be able to get a meal.

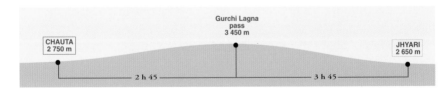

The Sixth Day

FROM JHYARI TO LAKE RARA (about 2 hours and 30 minutes)
After the village, follow a forest path climbing along the ridge of a hill for an hour. You will soon reach a flat grassland area scattered with pine trees. It will take you thirty minutes to cross this plateau, at the end of which you will have your first glimpse of the lake. Go down and follow its southern bank for an hour until you reach a long wooden bridge across the Nijar Khola, one of the rivers which has its source in the lake. The path on the left follows the stream for about fifteen minutes and leads to Maghghatta.

You will find two restaurants offering the local food - dal bhat, potatoes and black tea. You can camp on the grass nearby. However, if you have your own food it will be better to camp by the lake, where there are special sites for tourists.

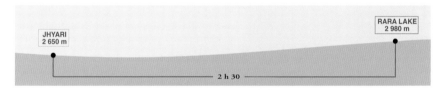

JHYARI
2 650 m

RARA LAKE
2 980 m

2 h 30

Camping on top of the roof of the Maghghatta Lodge.

The Seventh Day

Around Lake Rara

With a circumference of about 15 kilometres, Lake Rara, also called Rara Daha, is Nepal's largest lake, though not the highest as it is only at an elevation of 2,980 metres. Oval in shape, it is framed by Gurchi Lekh (4,607 metres) to the south, and Chankheli Lekh (4,201 metres) towards the north. The surrounding hills are covered with forests of rhododendron and pine.

For a long time, the place was used as a summer residence by the princes of the Malla dynasty (see page 14). All that remains of this era are a few steles near the park-keeper's house. Two communities, who once lived on the west bank of the lake until the creation of the National Park in 1975, were shifted to another part of the Terai. A small temple, dedicated to Lord Mahadev, is all that remains of the deserted villages of Rara and Chhapru.

Except for the guards and soldiers who are responsible for the surveillance of the area there are no permanent inhabitants. Going around the lake takes the whole day and you are very likely to come across an army encampment, which is off limits and

The Mahadev temple, in the ruins of Chhapru.

is of little interest anyway. There is a small grocery shop where you can buy anything from soaps to biscuits and batteries.

More interesting is the walk which leads to the top of Murma Peak, not mentioned on any map but which offers the best view of the lake. Leave early in the morning towards the direction of Maghghatta hamlet. Carry on westwards until the village of Murma, about an hour away. The path disappears amidst cultivated fields so just continue until you reach the top (3,500 metres). The view of Lake Rara with the surrounding peaks reflected in its waters is just superb. Further away you can see the foothills of Saipal (7,050 metres).

The Eighth Day

FROM LAKE RARA TO BOTA (about 6 hours and 45 minutes)
Go down the hill and follow the Nijar Khola for about fifteen minutes until you find two small wooden bridges that you will have to cross. Ignore the path on the right which leads to the village of Sikdi. Instead, take the path which climbs through the middle of a pine forest.

It will take you two hours to reach the Chuchemara Danda Pass, 3,800 metres high. The only water available on this part of the route is a small source just before the pass, but it may be dry. However, you have a superb view of Lake Rara and the Himalayan range.

Follow the path below the ridge of the hill for thirty minutes before you start going down a steep slope. After a few shepherds' huts the slope becomes gentle but it still takes an hour to reach the bottom of the valley and enter a vast pasture where goats and sheep usually graze. You are not too far from the hamlet of Ghorsina where there is an army base but no one will check your trekking permit. Follow the stream for forty five minutes and you will reach another plateau irrigated by the Ghatte Khola. It will take you about thirty minutes to cross this plateau.

Double terraced houses in Bota.

At the end of it starts an hour long, tough descent down a rocky path which will lead you to several grain-mills gathered along the stream. At the junction, take the path on your left and climb the hill for fifteen minutes. You will soon see the big village of Bota, huddled at the bottom of a small valley. Once again there are no lodges and you will have to arrange for your own accommodation for the night with the local inhabitants.

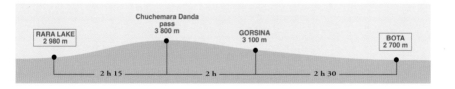

RARA LAKE 2 980 m — Chuchemara Danda pass 3 800 m — GORSINA 3 100 m — BOTA 2 700 m

2 h 15 — 2 h — 2 h 30

The Ninth Day

FROM BOTA TO MASHADHANI (about 4 hours and 30 minutes)
Walk towards the west to return to the Sinja Khola. At this point, the river flows
through very deep gorges and for two hours you will have to follow a path which
overlooks the northern bank and leads to the large valley of Sinja. Though the
path is a series of ups and downs, it is somehow an enjoyable walk. After the
gorges, you will see several caves in the hillside and a little later, a small, shaky
bridge which crosses the Sinja Khola and faces the caves. Unless you want to
have lunch in Sinja, you don't have to go into the village. In any case, as there are
no bhattis or restaurants in Sinja, you would have to eat at someone's house once
again.

After you have crossed the bridge, go up to the hamlet of Saubara, about
thirty minutes away. From the path you can see the tin roofs of the Kanaka
Sundari temple (Sundari means very beautiful), dedicated to a goddess similar to
the Kumari of Kathmandu. Unlike Kathmandu, however, some animals are
sacrificed here.

From Saubara, follow the southern bank of the Jaljala Khola. Two hours later
you should reach another bridge which will take you to the northern side,
towards the hamlet of Mashadhani (2,800 metres), the last inhabited place before
the path goes to Jumla. The local people walk from Sinja to Jumla at one stretch,
in less than eight hours. However, it is better for occasional trekkers to camp in
Mashadhani so as to conserve their energy.

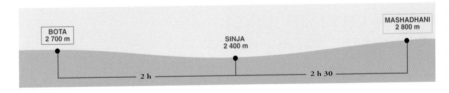

The Tenth Day

FROM MASHADHANI TO JUMLA (about 7 hours)
A few minutes after Mashadhani, you will come to a junction. Take the path
going towards the Jaljala Khola and cross the wooden bridge over it. Once on the
southern bank climb for forty five minutes through a forest until you reach an

open space. Go down again for fifteen minutes and cross another river. From here the path is relatively flat for about an hour, until it reaches some pastures at Chhala Chaur or 'buffalo leather'. According to legend, the gods killed a buffalo who went on a rampage destroying trees, and spread its skin over this spot.

A steep climb lasting for at least an hour will lead you to another larger pasture called Jaljala (which means 'swamp'), followed by another grassland called Gath Malla. All these places have grass, water and wood (please use the wood sparingly) and are perfect camping sites if you are carrying food.

It will take you an hour to reach the Bandhari Malla Pass from Gath Malla and yet another hour to reach the Deorali Chauri Khola where you will find a restaurant to have lunch in. The sign is only written in Nepali but you can easily identify it by the small model of an airplane hanging from its roof.

During the five-hour journey from Mashadhani to the Deorali Chari Khola, there is not a single place where food is available. This amply proves how important it is to carry your own provisions.

From the Deorali Chauri Khola, follow the ridge of a hill for thirty minutes, up to a large pasture from where you can have your first glimpse of Jumla and its surrounding mountains. Then the slope becomes steeper and it takes an hour to reach a technical school which you can hardly miss. You are now in the 'suburb' of Jumla, fifteen minutes away from the city centre.

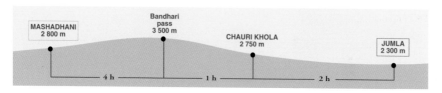

The Eleventh Day

AROUND JUMLA

We had reserved the last day for visiting the surroundings of Jumla only because some unforeseen event might delay the whole trip. Also the flight back to Nepalgunj needs to be reconfirmed, and it is wiser to plan for an extra day between the day the trek ends and the day you take off. You could also take advantage of this surplus time to climb Mount Chimara, overlooking Jumla from a height of 3,724 metres.

Go in the direction of the airport and after the control tower head eastwards towards the hamlet of Danshangu. The ascent will take you three hours if you are fast, five hours if you want to do it leisurely. The difference in altitude levels makes it difficult to follow the path. After the first foothills, the path goes through large grasslands. It soon becomes more and more steep as it enters rocky terrain. You will notice three small peaks marked with cairns. The fourth one, with an old temple, is the topmost. Although in ruins, the Hindu temple of Bhagawati is revered by everyone in the region. If you follow the ridge you will soon come across the new telephone exchange building.

From the top of Chimara, you can not only see the entire Jumla Valley, but also the different routes leading to Lake Rara, which nicely rounds off the trek.

Those who prefer a more relaxing day can walk along the Tila Nadi River and visit some relics of the Malla dynasty. Via the village of Micha, it is possible to reach the hot springs of Tatopani in four hours. The so-called hot springs are in fact dirty ponds of sulphurous water used by the villagers to wash clothes. Taking a bath is not recommended but it is worth the trip for the ambience.

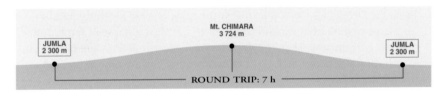

Acknowledgements

I would like to thank Shiva Raja Joshi, Danu Simigaon Sherpa, Birkhasing Tamang and Ram Kumar Nepali who escorted me through my peregrinations across Nepal. Without their help, their patience, their experience and their friendship, I would never have been able to write this book.

I also want to thank all the Nepalis I met, whose names I have forgotten but whose faces and memories will always remain in my mind, as one never completely forgets the mountains.

Part Three: Glossary

Prayer wheels: tradition and resourcefulness

Nepali and Tibetan Terms

Annapurna: Goddess of Abundance. One of the main mountains in Nepal is named after her.

baksheesh: more or less the equivalent of a tip...or a bribe.

bazaar: market.

bhatti: small local café.

Bhotia: A general term for Tibetan-influenced people of the northern border regions.

Bon: Tibet's ancient religion. A complex mixture of animism and magic.

Brahman: the highest caste of the Hindu caste system. According to the tradition, Brahmans come from the mouth of the god Brahma.

cairn: small mound of stones used to show the way.

chang: locally brewed beer.

chautara: a kind of stone bench used by porters to rest in the shade.

Chhetri: the second 'purest' caste. Chhetris belong to the caste of warriors and are supposed to be born from the arms of Brahma.

chorten: Buddhist altar. The eyes of the Buddha are painted on the four walls of the sanctuary. The nose is represented by the number 1, which is the symbol of unity.

dablam: reliquary necklace worn by Sherpa women.

Dalai Lama: spiritual and temporal ruler of Tibet. The current Dalai Lama lives in exile in India ever since China took over Tibet.

danda: top of a ridge.

danphe: Impeyan pheasant with colourful feathers. Emblem of Nepal.

deurali (or deorali): low altitude pass.

doko: large rattan basket carried by porters.

prayer flags: pieces of material printed with prayers which the wind is supposed to take to the gods.

gompa: Buddhist monastery.

guru: spiritual master.

himal: mountain.

kang: mountainain (in Tibetan)

kani: stone doorway found at the entrance of a village.

khola (or kosi): river.

khukri: large knife with a curved blade. Used in the fields as well as to sacrifice **animals**. A good quality khukri must have a small notch at the base of the blade so that blood does not stain the hilt.

Kumari: young virgin considered as a Living Goddess.
kund: lake (in Hindi)
la: high altitude pass (in Tibetan)
lama: Buddhist priest.
lodge: kind of 'bed and breakfast'.
mani: stone engraved with a mantra. Traditionally, Buddhists pile them one on top of the other to build small walls called mani walls. Always walk around them keeping the stones on your right side.
mantra: sacred formula repeated continuously during prayers.
moraine: rocky area at the base of a glacier.
pokhari: pond or small lake.
raksi: local alcohol.
saligram: fossil mollusc commonly found in the high valley of the Kali Gandaki. Evidence of an ancient sea in the middle of the Himalayan range. Hindus consider it a symbol of Lord Vishnu.
sirdar: guide.
tahr: wild goat.
tal: lake.
Thakuri: ancient dynastynow a sub-branch of the Chhetri caste.
thangka: sacred painting.
trishul: trident. One of the symbols of Lord Shiva.
tsho: lake (in Tibetan)
yak: large local bovine, bred for its milk, wool and to carry loads.
yeti: some believe it to be a huge monkey; others consider it to be a mythical monster. Supposed to reside in the Khumbu region.

Instant Nepali

Nepali is more difficult to pronounce than the basic transliteration used here would have you believe. There are four different ways of enunciating the sound indicated by 'D'- retroflex, aspirated, aspirated retroflex, and the 'normal' English version. The same goes for 'T'. There are the aspirated consonants, and long and short vowels. To avoid confusion, the simplest transliteration is used here.

Hello	Namaste (Namaskar to indicate great respect)
Goodbye	Namaste or
	bistari januhos (to someone departing)
	ramro sangha basnuhos (to someone staying)
See you again	feri betaunla
Yes/no	ho/hoina, cha/chaina
There is (are)/isn't (aren't)	cha/chaina
Do you speak English?	Tapai Inglis bolnu huncha?
I don't understand	Ma bujdaina.
Pardon?	Hajur?
Excuse me.	Maph garnuhos.

'Please' is built into verb forms; only the polite forms are shown here. 'Thank you' is translated as dhanyabad, but it's not applied as indiscriminately as in English. Routine thanks for all but the most exceptional transactions is best conveyed by a smile and a nod, or even 'tenk you'.

SHOPPING

Where can I get (bananas)?	(Kera) kaha paincha?
How much is this?	Yesko kati?
How much altogether?	Jama kati bhayo?
That's expensive.	Derey mahango cha.
A little cheaper, please.	Ali sastoma dinuhos.
good	ramro
no good	naramro
I like it	malai man parcha
I don't like it	malai man pardaina
don't need, don't want	malai chaindaina
money	paisa
change	chanchun

NUMBERS

one .... ek
two .... dui
three .... teen
four .... char
five .... panch
six .... cha
seven .... sat
eight .... at
nine .... nau
ten .... das
twenty .... bis
thirty .... tis
forty .... chalis
fifty .... pachas
sixty .... sathi
seventy .... satari
eighty .... awsi
ninety .... nabbey
one hundred .... ek say
one thousand .... ek hajar

DAYS OF THE WEEK

Sunday .... aitabar
Monday .... sombar
Tuesday .... mangalbar
Wednesday .... budhabar
Thursday .... bihibar
Friday .... sukrabar
Saturday .... sanibar

USEFUL WORDS

here/there .... yaha/tyaha
this/that .... yo/tyo
yesterday/today/tomorrow .... hijo/aja/bholi
morning/afternoon/evening/night .. bihana/diuso/beluka/rati
day/week/month/year .... din/hapta/mahina/sal, barsa
before/after .... aghi/pachi

fast/slow .... chito/bistari
a little/a lot .... ali-ali, ali kati/dherai
the same/another (one) .... yotai/arko
big/small .... thulo/sano
cheap/expensive .... sasto/mahango
clean/dirty .... safa/pohor
hot/cold (person, weather) .... garam/jado
hot/cold (liquid) .... tato/chiso
difficult/easy .... gadho, aptyaro/sajilo
near/far .... najik/tada
new/old .... naya/purano
open/closed .... kholeko/bhanda
uphill/downhill .... ukalo/oralo
cold .... jado lagyo
hot .... garmi lagyo
hungry .... bhok lagyo
thirsty .... tirka lagyo
tired .... takai lagyo
lazy .... alchi lago
pleasant, nice .... ramailo lagyo
happy .... kushi lagyo

FOOD .... khana

rice .... bhat
rice and lentils .... dal bhat
cooked vegetables .... tarkari, subji
potatoes .... alu
greens .... sag
spicy .... piro
not spicy, please .... piro nabanaunuhos
chilli .... khursani
noodles .... chow-chow
bread (unleavened/leavened) .... roti/pau roti
snack .... khaja
meat .... masu
chicken .... khukhurako masu
buffalo .... rungako masu
goat .... khasiko masu
fish .... macha

egg .... phul, anda
fruit .... phalphul
orange .... suntala
apple .... syau
banana .... kera
yoghurt .... dahi
tasty .... mitho
candy .... mithai
milk .... dudh
soft drink .... chiso (kok, fanta, eesprite)
beer .... biyar
local liquor .... raksi
coffee .... kafi
tea .... chiya
milk tea .... dudh chiya
black tea .... kalo chiya
lemon tea .... kagati chiya
no sugar please .... chini nahalnuhos
drinking water .... khaney pani
boiled water .... umaleko pani

PEOPLE

An endearing feature of Nepali is the way kinship terms are used to address strangers. When addressing someone roughly your age, say 'didi' or 'dai/daju' (older sister/brother). Older people are amai or bajey; younger bahini or bhai. Shopkeepers are sahuni (female) or sahuji (male) - literally, 'wealthy one'.

boy .... keta
girl .... keti
kids (offspring) .... bacha
(in general) .... keta-keti
son .... chora
daughter .... chori
husband .... sriman or logney
wife .... srimati or patni (formal), or
                                                        swasni (informal)
(my) mother .... (mero) ama
(your) father .... (tapaiko) ba
(his/her) friend .... (wahako) sathi

USEFUL PHRASES

How are you?	Tapailai kasto cha?
What's the matter/ what happened?	Ke bhayo?
What's your name?	Tapaiko nam ke ho?
Where do you live?	Tapai kaha basnu huncha?
How old are you?	Tapaiko umer kati?
Are you married?	Tapaiko biha bhayo?
What kind of work do you do?	Tapai ke kam garnu huncha?
I speak only a little Nepali.	Ma Nepali ali-ali matrai bolchu.
I don't know.	Malai taha chaina.
Where is this bus going?	Yo bas kaha jancha?
What time will we reach Kathmandu?	Kathmanduma kati bajey pugcha?
What time do we go?	Kati bajey jancha?
What time is it now?	Ahiley kati bajyo?
Taxi! Are you empty?	Tyaksi! Khali ho?
How much to go to Bhaktapur?	Bhaktapurma janey kati parcha?
Where is?	kaha cha?
Which is the trail to Sankhu?	Sankhu janey bato kun chahi ho?

TREKKING

How many hours to reach the next town?	Pallo gau pugnalai kati ghanta lagcha?
What's the name of this town?	Yo gauko nam ke ho?
Is there a place to stay?	Basne thau cha? or bas paincha?
Please show me a room.	Kota dekaunuhos na.
Is there anything better/ cheaper/bigger than this?	Yo bhanda ramro/sasto/thulo cha?
One person only	Ek jana matrai
Two people	dui jana
My friend is coming	Mero ek jana sathi auncha.
Where can I get some food?	Khana kaha paincha?

Finally, the two most frequently asked questions encountered on the trail:

Where are you going?	Kaha janu huncha?
Where are you coming from?	Kaha bata aunu bhaeko?

Recommended Reading

Travel and Description

Greenwald, Jeff. Shopping for Buddhas (Harper & Row, 1990). Amusing personal account of Western consumers in hot pursuit of Eastern spirituality.

Herzog, Maurice. Annapurna (Jonathan Cape, 1952). The story of the first successful ascent of an 8,000-metre peak (finding the mountainain was a problem). That adventure pales in comparison to the harrowing saga of the long, painful return journey (Herzog's fingers and toes were severely frostbitten so most had to be amputated along the trail). A gripping story, told with great dignity.

Iyer, Pico. Video Night in Kathmandu (Knopf, 1988). A romp through the Eastern tourism scene. The chapter on Kathmandu is not the strongest, but the book captures the bizarre mutations that occur when East meets West.

Matthiessen, Peter. The Snow Leopard (Viking, 1978). A luminous modern masterpiece that has probably inspired more visits to Nepal than any other book. Matthiessen accompanied zoologist George Schaller on a trip to the remote Himalayan region of Dolpo in search of the rare snow leopard. This is at once a description of the trek, and of the author's inner journey.

Peissel, Michel. Mustang: A Lost Tibetan Kingdom (Collins and Harvill Press, 1968). The adventurous Tibetan-speaking author became one of the few Westerners to penetrate the restricted region of Mustang with his 1964 visit.

Pye-Smith, Charlie. Travels in Nepal (Aurum Press, 1988). Blending good travel writing with keen observations on various projects and issues, this book is a palatable way of diving into the complexities of development in Nepal.

Snellgrove, David L. Himalayan Pilgrimage (Oxford, 1961). Account of the Buddhist scholar's 1956 journey through Dolpo, the Kali Gandaki and Manang. Fascinating insights into how it was, permeated with dry humour.

Thapa, Manjushree. Mustang Bhot in Fragments (Himal Books, 1992). Daughter of a Nepali diplomat, Thapa grew up in America and returned to Nepal as both insider and outsider. This slim volume records her observations on two visits to the newly-opened Mustang region.

Tilman, H. W. Nepal Himalaya (Cambridge University Press, 1952). Reprinted in The Seven Mountainain-Travel Books, (The Mountaineers 1983). Tilman was an old hand by the time he went on this 1949 excursion, the first reconnaissance of the Langtang, Annapurna and Everest regions, but his sense of humour is as wry and sharp as ever.

Tucci, Giuseppe. Journey to Mustang (Reprinted by Ratna Pustak Bhandar, 1977). Essential reading for the trek to Muktinath: the celebrated Tibetologist's 1952 journey up the Kali Gandaki - his observant eye missing nothing along the way. The book is filled with both cultural insights and compassion.

People

Avedon, John. In Exile From the Land of Snows (Alfred A. Knopf, 1984). The heartbreaking story of Tibetans in exile, and the single best introduction to the Tibetan issue.

Chorlton, Windsor. Cloud-dwellers of the Himalayas: The Bhotia. (Time-Life Books, 1982). Superb photo essays and chapters documenting life in the remote valley of Nar-Phu, north of Manang. The life and customs described here apply to many Bhotia peoples.

Coburn, Broughton. Nepali Aama: Portrait of a Nepalese Hill Woman (Moon Publications, 1990). Black-and-white photos and quotes create a lovely, insightful documentary of an old and very spunky Gurung woman with whom the author lived as a Peace Corps volunteer.

Downs, Hugh R. Rhythms of a Himalayan Village (Harper & Row, 1980). A sensitive look at life in the Sherpa region of Solu, blending black-and-white photos, narrative and quotations.

Fisher, James F. Sherpas: Reflections on Change in Himalayan Nepal (Oxford University Press, 1990). Thoughts on changing Sherpa culture by an observer who first visited Khumbu in the early 1960s. Notable for the extent it allows Sherpas to speak for themselves.

Fürer-Haimendorf, Christoph von. Himalayan Traders (John Murray, 1975). Broad examination of Tibetan-oriented trading communities across the Nepal Himalaya and how their lives have changed with the advent of modern times.

Macfarlane, Alan, and Indra Bahadur Gurung. Gurungs of Nepal (Ratna Pustak Bhandar, 1990). This slim volume on modern Gurung life makes good reading for trekking in the Annapurna region.

History and Culture

Anderson, Mary M. The Festivals of Nepal (Unwin Hyman, 1971). The standard classic, though somewhat outdated. Engagingly written descriptions of major and minor festivals of the Kathmandu Valley.

Bista, Dor Bahadur. *Fatalism and Development: Nepal's Struggle for Modernisation* (Longman, 1990). A provocative examination of how the 'culture of fatalism' embedded in the Hindu caste hierarchy has hampered Nepal's development. The author's jaundiced look at the dominant culture has been severely censured by Brahmin Chhetri critics; the only way he can get away with it is being a Chhetri himself, and a respected anthropologist.

Farwell, Byron. *The Gurkhas* (Allen Lane, 1984). The history of the fearless Nepalese mercenaries who are often called the world's finest infantrymen.

Goodman, Jim. *Guide to Enjoying Nepalese Festivals* (Pilgrim Book House, 1993). Excellent summary of festivals in the Kathmandu Valley, with handy notations on what occurs when and where.

Landon, Percival. *Nepal* (Constable, 1928). Detailed two-volume set examining the history of the Valley, interesting for period notes but marred by the author's obsequious attitude towards his Rana hosts.

Levy, Robert I. *Mesocosm: Hinduism and the Organization of a Traditional Newar City in Nepal* (University of California, 1990). An incredibly complex, detailed study of the traditional Newari society of Bhaktapur, with special emphasis on spatial relations.

Sever, Adrian. *Nepal Under the Ranas* (Oxford University Press, 1993). Comprehensive, balanced survey of 104 years of Rana rule, well-written and illustrated with rare historic photographs.

Slusser, Mary. *Nepal Mandala: A Cultural Study of the Kathmandu Valley* (Princeton University Press, 1982). Massive (and expensive) two-volume study of the Valley's Newari culture and its unique blending of Buddhist and Brahmanical traditions, both serious and fascinating.

Whelpton, John. *Jang Bahadur in Europe.* (Sahayogi Press, 1983). An entertaining account of the Prime Minister's 1850 visit to England and France, including a translation of a narrative written by a member of the party.

Religion

Anderson, Walt. *Open Secrets: A Western Guide to Tibetan Buddhism* (Viking, 1979). Accessible look at Tibetan Buddhism, emphasising its psychological aspects.

O'Flaherty, Wendy Doniger (editor). *Hindu Myths* (Penguin, 1975). Wide selection of the essential Hindu myths which permeate Nepalese art and religion.

Sogyal Rinpoche. *The Tibetan Book of Living and Dying* (Harper, San Francisco, 1992). A lucid and inspiring account of Tibetan Buddhism by an Oxford-educated lama.

Stutley, Margaret. Hinduism: The Eternal Law (The Aquarian Press, 1985). Basic introduction to Hindu literature, deities and beliefs.

Art

Aran, Lydia. The Art of Nepal (Sahayogi Prakashan, 1978). A remarkably relevant study of Nepalese art, focusing on the Kathmandu Valley and doubling as a study of religious iconography.

Bernier, Ronald. The Nepalese Pagoda - Origins and Style (S. Chand, 1979). This scholarly yet readable examination of the complex symbolism embedded in Nepalese temples adds much depth to Valley sightseeing.

Macdonald, Alexander W., and Anne Vergati Stahl. Newar Art: Nepalese Art during the Malla Period (Vikas, 1979). Architecture and paintings of the Kathmandu Valley examined in the context of classical Newari culture.

Pal, Pratapaditya. Art of Nepal (University of California Press, 1985). Catalogue of the Los Angeles County Museum's marvellous collection of Nepalese art.

Natural History

Cameron, Ian. Mountainains of the Gods (Century, 1984). An illustrated survey of the Himalaya, its history, geology, ecology and peoples.

Fleming, Dr Robert L., Jr. and Lain Singh Bangdel. Birds of Nepal (Nature Himalayas, 1976). The standard classic, with colour illustrations of 1,000 individuals of 753 species accompanied by lucid descriptions for easy identification.

Gurung, K.K. Heart of the Jungle: The Wildlife of Chitwan Nepal (André Deutsch, 1983). Well-written account of the natural history of Chitwan National Park.

Hillard, Darla. Vanishing Tracks: Four Years Among the Snow Leopards of Nepal (William Morrow, 1989). Enjoyable story of the first study of the endangered snow leopard, focusing on the cultures as well as the environment of the Western Nepal Himalaya.

Mishra, Hemanta R., and Margaret Jeffries. Royal Chitwan National Park: Wildife Heritage of Nepal (The Mountainaineers, 1991). A thorough guidebook to the flora, fauna and people of Chitwan.

Trekking and Rafting

Bezruchka, Stephen. A Guide to Trekking in Nepal. (The Mountainaineers, 1985). The classic trekkers' guide: thorough, sincere and responsible, with detailed trail descriptions of 40 different routes and in-depth sections on culture, language and health.

Duff, Jim and Peter Gormley. The Himalayan First Aid Manual (World Expeditions, 1992). Handy pocket-sized guide to doctoring yourself and others on the trail. Available at the HRA office in Kathmandu.

Hayes, John L. Trekking North of Pokhara (Roger Lascelles, 1993). A brief essential guide to the most popular trekking region in Nepal.

Knowles, Peter and David Allardice. White Water Nepal: A Rivers Guidebook for Rafting and Kayaking (Rivers Publishing, 1992). The first guide to river rafting, written by experienced rafters. It's helpful in choosing a reliable commercial operator and in planning trips to remote areas.

McGuiness, Jamie. Trekking in the Everest Region (Trailblazer, 1993). Up-to-date, detailed guide to the Everest region; perfect if this is the only region you plan to visit.

Uchida, Ryohei. Trekking Mountain Everest (Chronicle Books, 1991). A souvenir rather than a guidebook, lavishly illustrated with colour photographs.

Fiction

Han Suyin. The Mountainain is Young (Jonathan Cape, 1958). Purple prose from the author of A Many-Splendoured Thing: a shy, sensitive Englishwoman, a 'wayward writer in search of herself', finds love in the Kathmandu of the early 1960s.

Robinson, Kim Stanley. Escape from Kathmandu (Tor, New York, 1989). An amusing romp through Everest, Yetis, trekking, lamas, Ranas, and other Nepal clichés.

Literature

Hutt, Michael James (translator and editor). Himalayan Voices (University of California, 1991). An eye-opening introduction to the riches of modern Nepali literature, both poetry and short stories.

Lienhard, Siegfried. Songs of Nepal (University of Hawaii Press, 1984). Anthology of Newari folksongs and hymns providing fascinating insights into culture and legends.

Rubin, David. Nepali Visions, Nepali Dreams (Columbia University Press, 1980). The translated poems of Lakshmi Prasad Devkota, considered Nepal's finest poet.

Photographic Studies

Gilman, Peter (editor). Everest: The Best Writing and Pictures from 70 Years of Human Endeavour (Little, Brown & Co., 1993). Magnificent photographs with a nice mix of essays excerpted from accounts of various encounters with the world's highest peak.

Kelly, Thomas L., and Patricia Roberts. Kathmandu: City on the Edge of the World (Abbeville Press), 1988. An in-depth look at the Valley's history, culture, festivals and people.

Valli, Eric, and Diane Summers. Dolpo: Hidden Land of the Himalayas (Aperture Foundation, 1987). Insightful, capturing the rhythms of life in a remote region.

-. Honey Hunters of Nepal (Thames & Hudson, 1988). Spectacular large-format book documenting the age-old honey extraction methods of the Gurungs of Central Nepal, who climb up sheer cliffs on rope ladders to boldly steal the honey from swarming bees.
Kathmandu Valley

Language

Clark, T. W. Introduction to Nepali (Ratna Pustak Bhandar, 1989). Formal, wide-ranging survey of grammar and vocabulary: one of the best books, and everything is in Romanized Nepali, which means you don't have to read the Devanagari script to learn the language.

Karki, Tika B., and Chij Shrestha. Basic Course in Spoken Nepali (Published by the authors, 1979). Peace Corps volunteers learn from this simple, situationally based book very good for hammering in the basics.

Meerdonk, M. Basic Gurkhali Dictionary (Straits Times Press, 1959). Handy pocket-sized volume with Nepali-English and English-Nepali.

Maps

Map of Nepal (1 : 1 500 000 scale), published by Nelles Verlag. Gives a general overview of the country and of its main roads. In addition, there is a map of the Kathmandu Valley and of the city, as well as maps of central and eastern Nepal (1 : 500 000 scale).

To go trekking the best maps are the topographical Schneider maps which indicate the relief and the differences of altitude.

* For Around the Annapurnas and The Annapurna Sanctuary treks: map no 9, Annapurna (1 : 100 000 scale)
* For Gosain Kund, Langtang & Helambu: map no 8, Helambu-Langtang (1 : 100 000 scale)
* For From Jiri to Namche Bazar: maps no 6, Tamba Kosi-Likhu Khola (1 : 500 000 scale) and no 5, Shorung/Hinku (1 : 50 000 scale).
* For The Everest Base Camp and The Gokyo Lakes: map no 2, Khumbu Himal (1 : 50 000 scale).
* There is no Schneider map for Lake Rara. However, you can try the map of Jomosom to Jumla & Surkhet, from the Mandala Trekking Maps series published in Kathmandu. Not of very good quality though and quite expensive.

INDEX OF PLACE NAMES

Notes